finger
food

finger food

LAUREL
GLEN

San Diego, California

Contents

Nibbles

Vegetable fries

1 lb. orange sweet potatoes
1 lb. beets
1 lb. parsnips
vegetable oil, for deep-frying

Preheat the oven to 350°F.

Run a vegetable peeler along the sweet potatoes and beets to make thin ribbons. Cut the parsnips into thin slices.

Fill a deep, heavy-bottomed saucepan one-third full of oil and heat to 375°F or until a cube of bread dropped into the oil browns in 10 seconds. Cook the vegetables in batches for 30 seconds or until golden and crisp, turning with tongs if necessary. Drain on crumpled paper towels and season with salt. Keep warm on a baking sheet in the oven and cook the remaining fries.

Makes a large bowl

Chorizo and tomato salsa

2 tablespoons olive oil
½ lb. chorizo sausage, finely chopped
4 cloves garlic, finely chopped
4 small celery stalks, finely chopped
2 bay leaves
1 red onion, finely chopped
2 teaspoons paprika
6 ripe tomatoes, peeled, seeded, and
   chopped
2 tablespoons tomato paste
2 5-oz. cans corn, drained
1 cup fresh cilantro leaves, roughly
   chopped
1 tablespoon sugar

Heat the oil in a large frying pan.
Add the sausage, garlic, celery,
bay leaves, onion, and paprika.
Cook, stirring, over medium heat
for 10 minutes.

Add the tomatoes, tomato paste,
and corn, and cook over high heat
for 5 minutes or until the tomatoes
are pulpy and the mixture is thick.

Remove the pan from the heat, stir in
the cilantro and sugar, and season.
Serve hot.

Makes 3 cups

Olive tapenade

2²/₃ cups Kalamata olives, pitted
2 cloves garlic, crushed
2 anchovy fillets in oil, drained
2 tablespoons capers in brine, rinsed
and squeezed dry
2 teaspoons chopped, fresh thyme
2 teaspoons Dijon mustard
1 tablespoon lemon juice
¼ cup olive oil
1 tablespoon brandy (optional)

Place the Kalamata olives, crushed garlic, anchovies, capers, chopped thyme, Dijon mustard, lemon juice, olive oil, and brandy in a food processor and process until smooth. Season to taste with salt and freshly ground black pepper. Spoon into a clean, warm jar, cover with a layer of olive oil, seal, and refrigerate for up to one week. Serve on bruschetta or with *mezes*, Middle Eastern appetizers.

Makes 1½ cups

Notes: When refrigerated, the olive oil may solidify, making it an opaque, white color. This is a property of olive oil and will not affect the flavor of the dish. Simply bring the dish to room temperature before serving and the olive oil will return to a liquid state. Hint: To make sure your storage jar is very clean, preheat the oven to 250°F. Wash the jar and lid thoroughly in hot, soapy water and rinse well with hot water. Put the jar on a baking sheet and place in the oven for 20 minutes or until fully dry. Do not dry the jar or lid with a dishcloth.

Crispy Asian noodle pancakes

5 oz. dried rice vermicelli noodles
¼ cup chopped, fresh cilantro
3 scallions, finely sliced
1 small red chili, finely chopped
1 lemongrass stalk, white part only, finely chopped
1 clove garlic, crushed
vegetable oil, for frying

Place the noodles in a bowl and cover with boiling water. Allow to rest for 5 minutes or until soft. Rinse under cold water, drain, and dry gently with paper towels.

Place the noodles in a bowl with the cilantro, scallions, chili, lemongrass, and garlic. Season to taste with salt and mix well.

Heat the oil in a heavy-bottomed pan and fry 2 tablespoons of the mixture in hot oil. Flatten with a spatula while cooking and fry until crisp and golden on both sides. Drain the pancakes on paper towels and sprinkle with salt.

Makes about 25

Warm crab and lemon dip

1/3 cup butter
2 cloves garlic, crushed
3 shallots, thinly sliced
1 teaspoon mustard powder
1/2 teaspoon cayenne pepper
1/2 cup whipping cream
2/3 cup cream cheese
1/2 cup grated cheddar
11-oz. can crabmeat, drained
2 tablespoons lemon juice
2 teaspoons Worcestershire sauce
3 teaspoons chopped, fresh tarragon
1/2 cup fresh breadcrumbs
1 tablespoon chopped, fresh parsley

Preheat the oven to 325°F.

Melt half the butter in a saucepan, then cook the garlic and shallots for 2–3 minutes or until just softened. Add the mustard powder, cayenne pepper, and whipping cream. Bring to a simmer and slowly whisk in the cream cheese, a little at a time. When the cream cheese is completely incorporated, whisk in the cheddar and allow to cook, stirring constantly, over very low heat for 1–2 minutes or until smooth. Remove from the heat and add the crabmeat, lemon juice, Worcestershire sauce, and 2 teaspoons of the tarragon. Season to taste with salt and pepper. Mix, then transfer to a small baking dish.

Melt the remaining butter in a small saucepan, add the breadcrumbs, chopped parsley, and remaining tarragon, and stir until just combined. Sprinkle over the crab mixture and bake for 15 minutes or until golden. Serve warm.

Makes 2 1/2 cups

Parmesan wafers

1¼ cups grated Parmesan
1 tablespoon all-purpose flour
2 tablespoons fresh thyme

Preheat the oven to 425°F. Line two baking sheets with baking parchment, and using a 2¾-inch cutter as a guide, draw circles on the paper. Turn the paper upside down on the baking sheets.

Toss the cheese and flour together in a bowl, then sprinkle 2 teaspoons of the mixture over 3–4 circles on the paper, spreading the mixture to the edge of each round. Sprinkle a few thyme leaves over each round.

Bake in batches for 3 minutes or until melted but not firm. Using a spatula, turn the rounds over and cook for a minute more or until they are firm and light golden. Remove each round from the baking sheet and drape over a rolling pin or bottle until cool. Repeat with the rest of the ingredients.

Makes 30

Spinach pâté

13-oz. bag spinach
2 tablespoons butter
$1/2$ teaspoon ground coriander
pinch of cayenne pepper
2 scallions, roughly chopped
1 clove garlic
$1/3$ cup blanched almonds
2 teaspoons white wine vinegar
$1/2$ cup sour cream

Remove the stems from the spinach. Wash the leaves, leaving them wet, and place them in a saucepan. Cover and cook for 2 minutes or until wilted, then drain, saving $1/4$ cup of the cooking liquid. Cool the spinach, then squeeze dry.

Melt the butter in a small saucepan. Add the coriander, cayenne pepper, scallions, garlic, and almonds, and cook until the scallions are tender. Allow to cool.

Place in a food processor and process until finely chopped. Add the spinach and process, gradually adding the cooking liquid and vinegar.

Stir in the sour cream and season well with salt and pepper.

Makes 1$1/2$ cups

Seasoned popcorn

¼ cup vegetable oil
⅔ cup popcorn kernels
3 tablespoons butter
⅔ cup finely chopped Kalamata olives
1 fresh bird's-eye chili, finely chopped
1 clove garlic, crushed
1 tablespoon chopped, fresh parsley
1 tablespoon chopped, fresh oregano
1 teaspoon grated lemon zest

Heat the oil in a large saucepan, add the popcorn kernels, and cover. Cook over medium heat, shaking occasionally, until the popping stops. Transfer to a large bowl and discard any unpopped kernels.

Melt the butter in a large frying pan and add the remaining ingredients. Mix, then toss through the popcorn. Serve warm.

Makes a large bowl

Greek-style feta and yogurt dip

1²/₃ cups mild feta
1 cup ricotta
2 tablespoons olive oil
3 cloves garlic, crushed
1 tablespoon lemon juice
¼ teaspoon cayenne pepper
³/₄ cup Greek yogurt
⅓ cup chopped, fresh mint
1 teaspoon chopped, fresh oregano
¼ cup pitted black olives, diced
1 small tomato, finely diced
1–2 teaspoons lemon zest, thinly
   sliced

Puree the feta, ricotta, oil, garlic, lemon juice, cayenne pepper, and half the yogurt in a blender or food processor until smooth. Stir in the remaining yogurt, mint, and oregano.

Transfer the dip to a serving bowl and top with the olives, tomato, and lemon zest.

Makes 4 cups

Cheese sticks

1¼ cups all-purpose flour
⅓ cup unsalted butter, chilled and
   chopped
¾ cup grated Gruyère
1 tablespoon finely chopped, fresh
   oregano
1 egg yolk
1 tablespoon sea salt flakes

Line two baking sheets with baking parchment. Put the flour and butter in a food processor and process in short bursts until the mixture resembles fine breadcrumbs. Add the Gruyère and oregano and process for 10 seconds or until just combined. Add the egg yolk and about 1 tablespoon water, then process until the dough just comes together.

Turn the dough out onto a lightly floured surface and gather into a ball. Form 2 teaspoons of dough into a ball, then roll out into a stick about 5 inches long and place on the baking sheets. Repeat with the remaining dough, then cover with plastic wrap and refrigerate for 15–20 minutes. Preheat the oven to 400°F.

Lightly brush the sticks with water and sprinkle with the sea salt flakes. Bake for 10 minutes or until golden. Cool on a wire rack and serve with dips or as part of an antipasto platter.

Makes 30

Storage: Cheese sticks will keep for up to a week in an airtight container.

Spicy pappadums

3 green cardamom seeds
1½ tablespoons coriander seeds
1 tablespoon cumin seeds
2 cloves
1 teaspoon black peppercorns
1 bay leaf, crushed
1 teaspoon ground mace
¼ teaspoon ground cinnamon
pinch of chili powder
vegetable oil, for deep-frying
24 large pappadums (Indian lentil
   flatbread), broken into quarters

Dry-fry the cardamom, coriander, and cumin seeds, cloves, peppercorns, and bay leaf for 2–3 minutes or until richly fragrant. Cool for 5 minutes, then grind to a fine powder. Stir in the mace, cinnamon, and chili powder.

Fill a wide, large saucepan one-third full of oil and heat to 350°F or until a cube of bread dropped into the oil browns in 15 seconds. Deep-fry the pappadum quarters, a few at a time, until crisp and golden. Drain on crumpled paper towels and sprinkle with the spice mix while still hot.

Makes a large bowl

Corn salsa with cumin

3 ears of corn
2 tablespoons olive oil
2 teaspoons ground cumin
2 jalapeño chilies, stems and seeds
  removed, diced
1/4 cup sun-dried tomatoes, diced
2 tablespoons lime juice
1/4 cup cilantro leaves, finely chopped
3 scallions, finely chopped

Preheat the oven to 400°F. Cut the kernels from the ears of corn with a sharp knife—you will need 2 cups.

Combine the corn with the oil, cumin, chilies, and 1/4 cup water, and place in a baking dish. Bake in the oven for 30 minutes or until the corn begins to brown slightly.

Combine the corn with the tomatoes, lime juice, cilantro, and scallions. Season to taste.

Makes 1 1/2 cups

Two-seed crackers

2 cups all-purpose flour
1 teaspoon baking powder
2 tablespoons poppy seeds
2 tablespoons sesame seeds
1/3 cup butter, chilled and chopped
1/2 cup ice water

Preheat the oven to 350°F. Line two baking sheets with baking parchment or brush lightly with oil. Sift the flour, baking powder, and 1/2 teaspoon salt into a bowl. Add the seeds and season with pepper. Stir to combine. Rub the butter into the flour with your fingertips until the mixture resembles fine breadcrumbs.

Make a well in the center and add almost all the water. Mix with a rubber spatula or palette knife, adding the remaining water if necessary, until the mixture comes together in soft beads.

Gather the dough into a rough ball. Handle the dough gently, and do not knead it. Divide the dough into two portions. Place one portion between two sheets of wax paper and roll to a thickness of 1/8 inch. Cover the other portion with plastic wrap until needed.

Using a 2 1/2-inch round cookie cutter, cut rounds from the dough. Prick all over with a fork and transfer to the baking sheets. Repeat with the remaining dough. Pile any dough trimmings together (do not knead) and gently reroll. Cut out more rounds. Bake for 20–25 minutes or until lightly golden. Transfer to a rack to cool. Store in an airtight container for up to five days.

Makes 30

White bean dip

2 13-oz. cans lima or cannellini
  beans, drained and rinsed
½ cup olive oil
⅓ cup lemon juice
3 cloves garlic, finely chopped
1 tablespoon finely chopped, fresh
  rosemary

Place the beans in a food processor
with the oil, lemon juice, garlic,
rosemary, and 1 teaspoon salt.
Process until smooth, then season
with cracked black pepper.

Makes 3 cups

Note: This dip improves with time, so
it can be made up to two days ahead.

Tortilla shards

2 tablespoons sweet paprika
¼ teaspoon cayenne pepper
vegetable oil, for deep-frying
8 large flour tortillas, cut into long
    triangles

Combine the paprika and cayenne pepper in a small bowl.

Fill a deep, heavy-bottomed saucepan one-third full of oil and heat to 350°F or until a cube of bread browns in 15 seconds. Drop the tortilla shards in the oil in batches and deep-fry until crisp. Drain on paper towels and sprinkle lightly with the paprika mix while still hot.

Serves 8–10

Basil and cheese grissini

¼-oz. packet active dry yeast
1 teaspoon sugar
4 cups all-purpose flour
¼ cup olive oil
¼ cup chopped, fresh basil
½ cup finely grated Parmesan
2 teaspoons sea salt flakes

Combine the yeast, sugar, and 1¼ cups warm water in a bowl and leave in a warm place for 5–10 minutes or until foamy. Sift the flour and 1 teaspoon salt into a bowl. Stir the yeast and oil into the flour to form a dough, adding a little more water if necessary.

Gently gather the dough into a ball and turn out onto a lightly floured surface. Knead for 10 minutes or until soft and elastic. Add the basil and Parmesan and knead for 1–2 minutes to combine evenly.

Place the dough in a lightly oiled bowl and cover with plastic wrap. Leave in a warm place for 1 hour or until doubled in volume. Preheat the oven to 450°F and lightly grease two large baking sheets.

Punch down the dough and knead for 1 minute. Divide into 24 portions and roll each portion into a 12-inch-long stick. Place on the sheets and brush with water. Sprinkle with the salt flakes. Bake for 15 minutes or until crisp and golden.

Makes 24

Curried nuts

4 cups mixed nuts (almonds, brazil
  nuts, pecans, macadamias,
  cashews)
1 egg white
2 tablespoons curry powder
1 teaspoon ground cumin

Preheat the oven to 300°F. Spread
the nuts in a single layer on a baking
sheet and roast for 10 minutes.

Whisk the egg white until frothy, then
add the nuts, curry powder, cumin,
and 1 teaspoon salt. Toss together
and return to the oven for another
10–15 minutes, then allow to cool.

Makes 4½ cups

Aioli with crudités

Aioli
4 garlic cloves, crushed
2 egg yolks
1 ¼ cups light olive or vegetable oil
1 tablespoon lemon juice
pinch of ground white pepper

12 asparagus spears, trimmed
12 radishes, trimmed
½ cucumber, seeded, halved
lengthwise, and cut into batons
1 head of Belgian endive, leaves
separated

For the aioli, place the garlic, egg yolks, and a pinch of salt in a food processor and process for 10 seconds. With the motor running, add the oil in a thin, slow stream. The mixture will start to thicken. When this happens you can add the oil a little faster. Process until all the oil is incorporated and the mixture is thick and creamy. Stir in the lemon juice and white pepper.

Bring a saucepan of water to a boil, add the asparagus, and cook for 1 minute. Remove and plunge into a bowl of ice water.

Arrange the asparagus, radish, cucumber, and Belgian endive decoratively on a platter and place the aioli in a bowl on the platter. The aioli can also be used as a sandwich dressing or as a sauce for chicken or fish.

Serves 4

Note: It is important that all the ingredients are at room temperature when making this recipe. Should the aioli start to curdle, beat in 1–2 teaspoons boiling water. If this fails, put another egg yolk in a clean bowl and very slowly whisk the curdled mixture into it, one drop at a time, then continue as above.

Mixed Asian chips

vegetable oil, for deep-frying
16 cassava crackers, broken into
  small pieces (see Note)
16 round wonton wrappers
16 small, uncooked, plain prawn
  crackers
1 sheet toasted nori, shredded

Fill a deep, heavy-bottomed
saucepan or deep-fryer one-third
full of oil and heat to 350°F or until a
cube of bread dropped into the oil
browns in 15 seconds.

Deep-fry the cassava pieces until
crisp. Remove with a slotted spoon
and drain on crumpled paper towels.
Repeat with the wonton wrappers
and prawn crackers.

When they are all cool, combine and
toss with the nori.

Makes a large bowl

Note: Cassava crackers are made
from the flour of the dried cassava
root. Available from Asian markets.

Guacamole

2 large, ripe avocados
2 tablespoons lime juice
1 tomato, seeded and finely diced
1 fresh red chili, finely chopped
2 tablespoons finely diced red onion
1 1/2 tablespoons chopped cilantro
  leaves
1 1/2 tablespoons sour cream
1 tablespoon olive oil
1/2 teaspoon ground cumin
pinch of cayenne pepper

Put the avocados and lime juice in a large bowl, then mash. Stir in the diced tomato, chili, onion, cilantro, sour cream, olive oil, and cumin. Season with cayenne pepper and some salt and pepper.

Spoon into a serving bowl and sprinkle with cayenne pepper.

Makes 2 cups

Pizza wheels

½ small red pepper, finely chopped
¼ cup chopped, fresh parsley
2 tablespoons chopped, fresh
  oregano
3½ oz. finely chopped ham or salami
½ cup grated cheddar
¼ cup tomato paste
2 sheets frozen puff pastry, thawed

Preheat the oven to 400°F.

Combine the red pepper, parsley,
oregano, ham, and cheese in a bowl.

Spread the tomato paste onto each
sheet of pastry, leaving a ¾-inch
border along one side, and sprinkle
the red pepper mixture over the top.
Roll up the pastry to enclose the
filling, leaving the plain edge until last.
Brush the edge lightly with water and
fold over to seal.

Cut each roll into ½-inch rounds and
place onto greased baking sheets.
Bake for 20 minutes or until golden.

Makes 48

Hummus

1 cup dried chickpeas
2 tablespoons tahini
4 cloves garlic, crushed
2 teaspoons ground cumin
1/3 cup lemon juice
3 tablespoons olive oil
large pinch of cayenne pepper
lemon juice, extra
olive oil, extra
paprika
chopped, fresh parsley

Soak the chickpeas overnight in 4 cups water. Drain and place in a large saucepan with 8 cups fresh water (enough to cover the chickpeas by 2 inches). Bring to a boil, then reduce the heat and simmer for 1 1/4 hours or until the chickpeas are very tender. Remove any impurities from the surface. Drain well, set aside the cooking liquid, and leave until cool enough to handle. Pick out any loose skins and discard.

Process the chickpeas, tahini, garlic, cumin, lemon juice, olive oil, cayenne pepper, and 1 1/2 teaspoons salt in a food processor until thick and smooth. With the motor still running, gradually add enough of the cooking liquid (about 3/4 cup) to form a smooth, creamy puree. Season with salt or extra lemon juice.

Spread onto a flat bowl or plate, drizzle with oil, sprinkle with paprika, and toss the parsley over the top. Serve with pita bread.

Makes 3 cups

Cheese, olive, and sun-dried tomato toasts

2 cups self-rising flour
1 cup grated cheddar
¼ cup freshly grated Parmesan
⅓ cup pine nuts
1 cup milk
1 egg, lightly beaten
2 tablespoons butter, melted
½ cup pitted black olives, chopped
¼ cup sun-dried tomatoes, finely
  chopped
⅓ cup grated cheddar, extra

Preheat the oven to 400°F. Lightly grease two 10½ x 3-inch oblong pans and cover the bases with nonstick baking parchment. Combine the flour, cheeses, and pine nuts in a bowl. Make a hollow in the center of the mixture.

Combine the milk, egg, butter, olives, and sun-dried tomatoes, pour into the hollow of the flour mixture, and stir to form a slightly sticky dough.

Divide the mixture between the pans. Smooth the surface and sprinkle with the extra cheese. Bake for 45 minutes or until cooked through when tested with a skewer. Leave in the pans for 5 minutes, then turn onto wire racks to cool.

Cut into ¼-inch slices and place on baking sheets lined with baking parchment. Bake for 15–20 minutes or until toasts are golden and crisp.

Makes about 50

Fava bean dip

1 cup dried fava beans (see Note)
2 cloves garlic, crushed
¼ teaspoon ground cumin
1½ tablespoons lemon juice
⅓ cup olive oil
2 tablespoons chopped, fresh
  Italian parsley
flatbread, for serving

Rinse the beans well, then place in a bowl, cover with 2 cups of water, and allow to soak overnight.

If using peeled beans, transfer them and their soaking water to a large, heavy-bottomed saucepan. If using unpeeled beans, drain, then add to the saucepan with 2 cups fresh water. Bring to a boil, cover, and simmer for 5–6 hours. Check the water level and add boiling water as needed to keep the beans moist. Do not stir, but shake the saucepan occasionally to keep the beans from sticking. Set aside to cool slightly.

Puree the contents of the saucepan in a food processor, then transfer to a bowl and stir in the garlic, cumin, and lemon juice. Gradually stir in enough olive oil to give a dipping consistency. As the mixture cools, it may become thick, in which case you can stir in a little warm water to return the mixture to dipping consistency.

Spread over a large dish and sprinkle with the parsley. Serve with the flatbread, cut into triangles.

Serves 6

Note: The fava beans can be the prepeeled white ones or the small, brown ones.

Potato skins

6 large potatoes, unpeeled
vegetable oil, for deep-frying

Preheat the oven to 415°F. Prick each potato with a fork and bake for 1 hour or until the skins are crisp and the flesh is soft. Turn once during this time.

Allow the potatoes to cool, then halve them and scoop out the flesh, leaving a thin layer of potato in each shell. Cut each half into three wedges.

Fill a deep, heavy-bottomed pan one-third full of oil and heat to 375°F or until a cube of bread browns in 10 seconds. Cook the potato skins in batches for 2 minutes or until crisp. Drain on paper towels. Sprinkle with salt and pepper.

Makes 36

Shrimp and green chili pâté

⅓ cup butter
2 cloves garlic, crushed
1 small green chili, seeded and
   chopped
1½ lbs. shrimp, peeled and deveined
1 teaspoon finely grated lime zest
1 tablespoon lime juice
2 tablespoons mayonnaise
2 tablespoons chopped cilantro
hot pepper sauce, to taste (optional)

Melt the butter in a large frying pan and add the garlic, chili, and shrimp. Cook over medium heat for 20 minutes or until tender.

Place the shrimp mixture into a food processor, add the lime zest and juice, and process until roughly chopped. Stir in the mayonnaise and cilantro, and season with the hot pepper sauce, salt, and pepper. Spoon into a serving dish.

Chill for at least 1 hour or until firm. Return to room temperature before serving.

Makes 1⅔ cups

Spiced soy crackers

1¼ cups all-purpose flour
¾ cup soy flour
½ teaspoon garam masala
½ teaspoon paprika
2½ tablespoons olive oil
2½ tablespoons lemon juice

Place the flours, garam masala, paprika, and ½ teaspoon salt in a food processor. Add the oil, lemon juice, and ½ cup water, and blend until the mixture comes together in a ball. Cover in plastic wrap and place in the refrigerator for 1 hour.

Preheat the oven to 315°F. Line three baking sheets with baking parchment. Cut the dough into 5 or 6 pieces, then roll each piece into rectangles as thinly as possible. Cut each piece into long, thin triangles (1½ x 4 inches). Place on the prepared baking sheets.

Bake for 20 minutes or until crisp and lightly browned. Serve with your favorite dip.

Makes 24

Baba ghanouj
(Turkish eggplant dip)

2 eggplants (2 lbs.)
3 cloves garlic, crushed
1/2 teaspoon ground cumin
1/3 cup lemon juice
2 tablespoons tahini
pinch of cayenne pepper
1 1/2 tablespoons olive oil
1 tablespoon finely chopped
  Italian parsley
black olives, to garnish

Preheat the oven to 400°F. Pierce the eggplants several times with a fork, then cook over an open flame for 5 minutes or until the skin is black and blistering, then place in a roasting pan and bake for 45 minutes or until the eggplants are very soft and wrinkled. Place in a colander over a bowl to drain off any bitter juices and allow to stand for 30 minutes or until cool.

Carefully peel the skin from the eggplants, chop the flesh, and place in a food processor with the garlic, cumin, lemon, tahini, cayenne, and olive oil. Process until smooth and creamy. Alternatively, use a potato masher or fork. Season with salt and stir in the parsley. Spread onto a flat bowl or plate and garnish with the olives. Serve with flatbread or pitas.

Makes 1 3/4 cups

Note: If you prefer, you can roast the eggplant in a 400°F oven for 1 hour or until very soft and wrinkled. "Baba ghanouj" is roughly translated into English as "poor man's caviar."

Fried chickpeas

1¼ cups dried chickpeas
vegetable oil, for deep-frying
½ teaspoon paprika
¼ teaspoon cayenne pepper

Soak the chickpeas overnight in plenty of cold water. Drain well and pat dry with paper towels.

Fill a deep saucepan one-third full of oil and heat to 350°F or until a cube of bread dropped into the hot oil browns in 15 seconds. Deep-fry half the chickpeas for 3 minutes. Remove with a slotted spoon, drain on crumpled paper towels, and repeat with the rest of the chickpeas. Partially cover the saucepan, as some of the chickpeas may pop. Don't leave the oil unattended.

Deep-fry the chickpeas again in batches for 3 minutes per batch or until browned. Drain well again on crumpled paper towels. Combine the paprika and cayenne pepper with a little salt and sprinkle the mixture over the hot chickpeas. Allow to cool before serving.

Serves 6

Taramosalata

5 slices white bread, crusts removed
1/3 cup milk
3 1/2-oz. can taram (mullet roe)
1 egg yolk
1/2 small onion, grated
1 clove garlic, crushed
2 tablespoons lemon juice
1/3 cup olive oil
pinch of ground white pepper

Soak the bread in the milk for
10 minutes. Press in a strainer to
extract any excess milk, then place
in a food processor with the taram,
egg yolk, onion, and garlic. Process
for 30 seconds or until smooth,
then add 1 tablespoon lemon juice.

While processing, slowly pour in
the olive oil. The mixture should be
smooth and of a dipping consistency.
Add the remaining lemon juice and
a pinch of white pepper. If the dip
tastes too salty, add another piece
of bread.

Makes 1 1/2 cups

Variation: Try smoked cod roe instead
of the mullet roe.

Marinated olives

¾ cup Kalamata olives
¾ cup green olives
¾ cup extra-virgin olive oil
2 sprigs fresh rosemary
½ tablespoon fresh thyme leaves
2 small, fresh red chilies, seeded
2 cloves garlic, bruised
1 large piece lemon peel
½ teaspoon fennel seeds
2 fresh thyme sprigs, extra

Place the olives, oil, rosemary, thyme, chilies, garlic, lemon peel, and fennel in a saucepan and warm over low heat. Transfer to a bowl and marinate overnight at room temperature.

Remove the olives from the oil with a slotted spoon and discard the herbs, reserving the oil. Add the extra thyme to the olives before serving.

Makes 2 cups

Note: Serve the oil with bread.

Hot Italian Bolognese dip

1 tablespoon olive oil
1 onion, finely chopped
2 cloves garlic, chopped
10 oz. ground beef
14-oz. can diced tomatoes
3 tablespoons tomato paste
1 tablespoon chopped, fresh basil
1 tablespoon chopped, fresh parsley
sour cream, to serve

Heat the oil in a frying pan, add the onion and garlic, and cook, stirring occasionally, over medium heat for 3 minutes or until the onion is soft. Add the beef and cook, stirring, for 5 minutes or until browned, pressing with a spoon or the back of a fork to remove any lumps.

Add the tomatoes, tomato paste, and basil. Bring to a boil, then reduce the heat and simmer for 15 minutes. Stir in the parsley and season to taste with salt and pepper.

Serve hot, topped with a generous dollop of sour cream.

Makes 3 cups

Note: This dip can also be served in a round loaf. Eat immediately so the bread stays crispy.

Pepper and almond bread

2 teaspoons black peppercorns
2 egg whites
$\frac{1}{3}$ cup superfine sugar
$\frac{3}{4}$ cup all-purpose flour
$\frac{1}{4}$ teaspoon ground ginger
$\frac{1}{4}$ teaspoon ground cinnamon
1 cup almonds

Preheat the oven to 350°F. Grease a 10½ x 3-inch oblong pan and line the bottom and sides with baking parchment. Lightly crush the peppercorns with the back of a metal spoon or in a mortar and pestle.

Beat the egg whites and sugar with an electric mixer for 4 minutes or until the mixture turns white and thickens. Sift the flour, ginger, and cinnamon, and fold in with the almonds and crushed peppercorns.

Spread the mixture into the pan. Bake for 35 minutes or until lightly browned. Cool in the pan for at least 3 hours before turning out onto a board. (At this stage, you can wrap the bread in aluminum foil and slice the next day.) Using a serrated knife, cut the bread into ⅛-inch slices. Place the slices in a single layer on baking sheets. Bake in a 300°F oven for 25–35 minutes or until the slices are dry and crisp. Allow to cool completely before serving.

Makes about 70 pieces

Note: To make traditional almond bread, simply remove the peppercorns.

Herbed cheese log

2 cups cream cheese, softened
1 tablespoon lemon juice
1 clove garlic, crushed
2 teaspoons chopped, fresh thyme
2 teaspoons chopped, fresh tarragon
1 tablespoon chopped, fresh
  Italian parsley
1 cup snipped, fresh chives

Put the cream cheese in a large bowl and beat with an electric mixer until soft and creamy. Mix in the lemon juice and garlic. In a separate bowl, combine the thyme, tarragon, and chopped parsley.

Line an 8 x 12-inch pan with aluminum foil. Spread the chives over the bottom of the pan, then spoon the cream cheese mixture over the chives. Using a flexible bladed knife, gently spread the mixture into the pan, pushing it into any gaps. Sprinkle the combined herbs evenly over the top.

Lift the aluminum foil from the pan and place on a work surface. Roll the cheese into a log, starting from the longest edge, then cover and place on a baking sheet. Refrigerate for at least 3 hours or preferably overnight.

Makes a 12-inch log

Honey-roasted peanuts

2¼ cups raw, shelled peanuts
½ cup honey
1½ teaspoons Chinese five-spice
    powder

Preheat the oven to 300°F.

Combine the ingredients in a small saucepan and warm over low heat.

Spread the nuts onto a large baking sheet lined with baking parchment and bake for 15–20 minutes or until golden brown. Cool before serving.

Makes 2½ cups

Storage: You can store the honey-roasted peanuts in an airtight container for up to a week.

Warm lentil dip

$^2/_3$ cup red lentils
1 tablespoon olive oil
1 onion, chopped
2 cloves garlic, crushed
2 teaspoons grated, fresh ginger
$^1/_2$ teaspoon ground turmeric
1 teaspoon ground cumin
14-oz. can diced tomatoes
1 tablespoon chopped, fresh cilantro

Wash the lentils under cold running water and drain well. Heat the oil in a large frying pan. Add the onion, garlic, and ginger, and cook over medium heat for 3–4 minutes or until the onion is soft and translucent.

Add the turmeric, cumin, and lentils, and cook, stirring, for 1 minute or until fragrant. Add 1 cup water and the undrained tomatoes to the mixture and bring to a boil, then reduce the heat and simmer for 20 minutes or until the lentils are soft.

Transfer the mixture to a food processor and process until well combined. Add the cilantro, season, and process until combined.

Makes 2 cups

Herbed lavash

½ cup olive oil
3 cloves garlic, crushed
6 slices lavash bread
2 teaspoons sea salt flakes
2 teaspoons dried, mixed Italian herbs

Preheat the oven 350°F.

Heat the oil and garlic in a small saucepan over low heat until the oil is warm and the garlic is fragrant but not browned.

Brush the lavash bread on both sides with the garlic oil. Cut each piece of bread into eight triangular wedges and position them side by side on baking sheets. Sprinkle with the sea salt and herbs. Bake for 8–10 minutes or until crisp.

Makes about 48 pieces

Pork and peanut dip

Paste
2 small, dried red chilies
2 teaspoons chopped, fresh
  cilantro root
3 teaspoons ground white pepper
6 cloves garlic, chopped
4 red Asian shallots, chopped

1 tablespoon peanut oil
10 oz. ground pork
2 fresh kaffir lime leaves
1 cup coconut cream
1/3 cup peanuts, toasted and chopped
1 1/2 tablespoons lime juice
3 tablespoons fish sauce
2 tablespoons brown sugar
1 tablespoon finely shredded, fresh
  Thai basil or cilantro leaves
peanut oil, for deep-frying
5 oz. cassava crackers

Place the chilies in a bowl of boiling water and soak for 15 minutes. Remove the seeds and chop. Blend all the paste ingredients in a food processor until smooth—add water if necessary.

Heat the oil in a saucepan. Add the paste and cook, stirring frequently, over medium heat for 15 minutes or until the paste darkens.

Add the ground pork and stir for 5 minutes or until it changes color. Gradually add the lime leaves and coconut cream, scraping the bottom of the saucepan. Cook for 40 minutes, stirring frequently, until almost all the liquid has evaporated. Add the peanuts, lime juice, fish sauce, and sugar, and cook for 10 minutes or until the oil begins to separate. Remove from the heat, discard the lime leaves, and stir in the basil.

Fill a deep, heavy-bottomed saucepan one-third full of oil and heat to 350°F or until a cube of bread browns in 15 seconds. Break the crackers in half. Deep-fry in small batches until pale and golden—they will puff up quickly, so remove immediately. Drain. Serve with the dip.

Serves 6–8

Dukkah

1/3 cup sesame seeds
1 tablespoon coriander seeds
2 teaspoons cumin seeds
1 teaspoon ground cumin
pinch of fennel seeds
1/2 teaspoon sea salt
1/2 teaspoon ground black
  peppercorns
1/2 cup blanched almonds, toasted

Combine the seeds, spices, salt, and peppercorns in a saucepan. Stir over low heat for 5 minutes or until the seeds are toasted. Cool completely.

Combine the almonds and seed mixture in the bowl of a food processor and process until the mixture resembles a coarse powder.

Serve with Turkish bread and olive oil for dipping.

Makes 3/4 cup

Green Mexican salsa

10-oz. can tomatillos, drained
  (see Note)
1 small onion, chopped
1 jalapeño chili, finely chopped
3 cloves garlic, crushed
2 tablespoons chopped cilantro
  leaves
1–2 teaspoons lime juice

Place the tomatillos in a food
processor with the onion, chili, garlic,
and 1 tablespoon of the cilantro.
Process until smooth, then blend in
the lime juice to taste. Add the rest
of the cilantro and process just long
enough to mix it evenly into the dip.

Makes 2 cups

Note: Tomatillos resemble green
tomatoes with a papery husk.
They are used extensively in
Mexican cooking.

Corn chips

4 corn tortillas
vegetable oil, for deep-frying

Cut each tortilla into eight pieces.

Fill a heavy-bottomed saucepan one-third full of oil and heat to 375°F or until a cube of bread dropped into the hot oil browns in 10 seconds. Cook the corn tortillas in batches for 1–2 minutes or until crisp and golden. Drain on crumpled paper towels. Sprinkle with salt, if desired.

Makes 32

Mini Indian yogurt bread

9-oz. packet Naan bread mix
  (see Note)
2 scallions, finely chopped
1 cup plain yogurt
1 tablespoon nigella seeds
  (black onion seeds)

Preheat the oven to 375°F. Empty the bread mix into a bowl and add the chopped scallions. Follow the manufacturer's instructions to make the dough.

Divide the dough into four portions, then divide each portion into six. On a lightly floured surface, roll each piece out to a 2-inch round.

Place the rounds on lightly greased baking sheets. Top with a teaspoon of yogurt, spread roughly, then sprinkle with the nigella seeds. Leave for 5 minutes. Bake for 15 minutes or until golden brown and crisp.

Makes 24

Note: Naan bread mix can be found in Indian or specialty markets.

Warm cheese dip

2 tablespoons butter
3 scallions, finely chopped
2 jalapeño chilies, finely chopped
$1/2$ teaspoon ground cumin
$3/4$ cup sour cream
2 cups grated cheddar
hot green pepper sauce, to drizzle

Melt the butter in a saucepan and add the scallions, chilies, and cumin. Cook without browning over low heat, stirring often, for 6–8 minutes.

Stir in the sour cream, and when it is warm, add the cheddar. Stir constantly until the cheese melts and the mixture is glossy and smooth. Transfer to a bowl, drizzle with a little pepper sauce, and serve warm.

Makes 2 cups

Spicy chicken goujons

3 boneless, skinless chicken breasts
all-purpose flour, for coating
vegetable oil, for deep-frying
1/2 teaspoon ground turmeric
1/2 teaspoon ground coriander
1/2 teaspoon ground cumin
1/2 teaspoon chili powder

Cut the chicken breasts into thin strips and toss in all-purpose flour, shaking off the excess.

Fill a deep, heavy-bottomed pan one-third full of oil and heat to 350°F or until a cube of bread dropped into the oil browns in 15 seconds. Cook the goujons in batches for 3 minutes or until golden. Drain on crumpled paper towels and keep warm.

Mix together the turmeric, coriander, cumin, chili powder, and 1 teaspoon salt. Toss the goujons in the mixture, shaking off the excess.

Makes about 30

Skordalia

1 lb. russet potatoes
5 cloves garlic, crushed
ground white pepper
$3/4$ cup olive oil
2 tablespoons white vinegar

Peel the potatoes and cut into $3/4$-inch cubes. Bring a large saucepan of water to a boil, add the potatoes, and cook for 10 minutes or until very soft.

Drain the potatoes and mash until quite smooth. Stir in the garlic, 1 teaspoon salt, and a pinch of ground white pepper. Gradually pour in the olive oil, mixing well with a wooden spoon. Add the vinegar and season to taste. Serve warm or cold with crusty bread or with barbecued meat, fish, or chicken.

Makes 2 cups

Notes: Do not make skordalia with a food processor—the processing will turn the potato into a gluey mess. Storage: Skordalia will keep in an airtight container for up to 2–3 days in the fridge. The potatoes will absorb the salt, so check the seasoning before serving.

Deep-fried cheese ravioli

vegetable oil, for deep-frying
10 oz. fresh cheese ravioli

Fill a deep, heavy-bottomed pan or deep-fryer one-third full of oil and heat to 350°F or until a cube of bread dropped into the oil browns in 15 seconds. Cook the ravioli in batches until golden brown.

Remove from the oil and drain on crumpled paper towels. Sprinkle with salt and cracked black pepper and serve hot.

Makes about 30

Note: Ideal with green Mexican salsa (see page 86). Also good on their own.

Roasted vegetable pâté

1 lb. orange sweet potatoes, peeled
and cut into chunks
1 red or yellow pepper, cut into
chunks
2 zucchini, sliced
3/4 lb. eggplants, cut into chunks
2 tomatoes, cut into chunks
8 scallions, cut into pieces
1 tablespoon extra-virgin olive oil
1 teaspoon sea salt
1 teaspoon grated lemon zest
2 tablespoons lemon juice

Preheat the oven to 425°F. Place the
vegetables in a large baking dish,
drizzle with oil, sprinkle with sea salt,
and roast for 45 minutes or until soft.

Transfer the vegetables to a food
processor and add the lemon zest
and lemon juice. Blend until smooth.
Spoon into a serving dish and cool
to room temperature.

Makes 4 cups

Herbed parchment bread

1 cup all-purpose flour
2 tablespoons extra-virgin olive oil
½ yellow onion, chopped
¼ cup fresh rosemary sprigs
¼ cup fresh parsley
¼ cup fresh mint leaves
2 teaspoons extra-virgin
  olive oil, extra
sea salt

Preheat the oven to 350°F. Process the flour and oil until the mixture resembles fine breadcrumbs. Transfer to a bowl.

Process the onion and herbs until finely chopped. Add 1 tablespoon of water and the extra oil and process until well combined. Add the herb mixture to the flour mixture and stir with a rubber spatula or flat-bladed knife until it starts to come together. Add an extra tablespoon of water, if needed. Press together and knead for 30 seconds.

Divide into sixteen pieces and roll each piece between two sheets of nonstick baking parchment as thinly as possible. Place on lightly greased baking sheets in a single layer. Lightly brush with water and sprinkle with sea salt.

Bake each sheet of breads for 8 minutes or until lightly browned and crisp to the touch. Transfer to wire racks to cool.

Makes 16

Tzatziki

2 small cucumbers (about ¾ lb.)
1²/₃ cups plain yogurt
4 cloves garlic, crushed
3 tablespoons finely chopped, fresh
   mint, plus extra to garnish
1 tablespoon lemon juice

Cut the cucumbers in half lengthwise.
Scoop out the seeds and discard.
Leave the skin on and coarsely grate
the cucumber into a small colander.
Sprinkle with salt and leave over a
large bowl for 15 minutes to drain
off any bitter juices.

Meanwhile, place the yogurt, crushed
garlic, the mint, and the lemon juice in
a bowl, and stir until well combined.

Rinse the cucumber under cold water.
Taking small handfuls, squeeze out
any excess moisture. Combine the
grated cucumber with the yogurt
mixture, then season to taste with
salt and freshly ground black pepper.
Serve immediately or refrigerate until
ready to serve, garnished with the
extra mint.

Makes 2 cups

Note: Tzatziki is often served as a
dip with flatbread, but is also suitable
to serve as a sauce to accompany
seafood and meat.
Storage: Tzatziki will keep in an
airtight container in the refrigerator
for 2–3 days.

Pesto bagel chips

4 plain bagels, three days old
½ cup pesto
1 cup shredded Parmesan

Preheat the oven to 325°F. Slice each bagel into six thin rings.

Bake the chips on a baking sheet for 10 minutes. Brush with pesto and sprinkle with shredded Parmesan. Bake for another 5 minutes or until the chips are lightly golden.

Makes 24

Layered Mexican dip

14-oz. can refried beans
1¼-oz. packet taco seasoning mix
10 oz. sour cream
1 quantity guacamole (see page 46)
6-oz. jar salsa (medium heat)
½ cup grated cheddar
1 tablespoon chopped cilantro

Combine the beans and the taco seasoning mix in a bowl.

Spread the bean mixture over the bottom of a serving plate, leaving a border on which to place the corn chips. Spread with the sour cream, then guacamole, then salsa, layering so you can see each separate layer. Sprinkle with the cheese and chopped cilantro.

Makes 7 cups

Note: This makes a large portion and is ideal for a large party. It can be assembled on a large, flat plate and surrounded by corn chips.

Parmesan puff straws

4 sheets frozen puff pastry, thawed
1/4 cup butter, melted
1 2/3 cups finely grated Parmesan
1 egg, lightly beaten

Preheat the oven to 400°F.

Lightly brush the pastry with the butter, then sprinkle each sheet with 1/4 cup of the cheese and season with salt and pepper. Fold each sheet in half, bringing the top edge down toward you. Brush the tops of each sheet with the egg. Sprinkle each with 2 tablespoons of extra grated Parmesan and season with salt.

Using a very sharp knife, cut the dough vertically into 1/2-inch-wide strips. Transfer each strip to a baking sheet lined with baking parchment, spacing them evenly. Hold each end of the pastry and stretch and twist in opposite directions. Bake in the oven for 10 minutes or until lightly browned.

Makes 80

Warm artichoke dip

2 13-oz. cans artichoke hearts,
    drained
1 cup mayonnaise
3/4 cup grated Parmesan
2 teaspoons onion flakes
2 tablespoons grated Parmesan,
    extra
ground paprika, to garnish

Preheat the oven to 350°F. Squeeze the artichokes to remove any liquid. Chop finely and combine with the mayonnaise, Parmesan, and onion flakes. Spread into a shallow, 4-cup flameproof dish.

Sprinkle with the extra Parmesan and paprika and bake for 15 minutes or until lightly browned and heated through. Serve hot.

Makes 4 cups

Ideas for dipping: Puff-pastry twists, crusty French bread.

Orange sweet potato wedges

2¾ lbs. orange sweet potatoes, peeled and sliced into 2½ x ¾-inch wedges
2 tablespoons olive oil
1 tablespoon fennel seeds
1 tablespoon coriander seeds
½ teaspoon cayenne pepper
1 teaspoon sea salt flakes

Preheat the oven to 400°F.

Place the sweet potatoes in a large baking dish and toss with the oil.

Using a mortar and pestle, pound together the fennel and coriander seeds until they are roughly crushed. Add to the orange sweet potatoes along with the cayenne and sea salt flakes. Toss well and bake for 30 minutes or until browned and crisp. Serve warm.

Serves 6–8

Parmesan, caper, and basil spread

1 cup low-fat cream cheese, softened
1/2 cup finely grated Parmesan
1 1/2 tablespoons capers, rinsed, dried, and roughly chopped
1 1/2 tablespoons finely chopped, fresh basil

Blend the cheeses in a bowl with a wooden spoon. Add the capers and basil. Season. Refrigerate for 1 hour to allow the flavors to develop.

Makes 1 1/4 cups

Ideas for dipping: Two-seed crackers (page 33), herbed parchment bread (page 102)

Crispy bread fingers

2 tablespoons sweet chili sauce
1 tablespoon peanut oil
1 loaf Turkish bread

Combine the sweet chili sauce and peanut oil.

Cut the bread in half. Brush the top and bottom with the oil mixture.

Place on a baking sheet and toast for 1–2 minutes or until crispy and golden. Cut into 3/4-inch fingers.

Makes about 50

Scallion flatbreads

2 teaspoons vegetable oil
2³/₄ cups thinly sliced scallions
1 clove garlic, crushed
¹/₂ teaspoon grated, fresh ginger
1³/₄ cups all-purpose flour
1¹/₂ tablespoons chopped cilantro
vegetable oil, for frying

Heat the oil in a frying pan and cook the scallions, garlic, and ginger for 2–3 minutes or until soft.

Combine the flour and 1 teaspoon salt in a bowl. Stir in the scallion mixture and the cilantro. Gradually stir in 1 cup boiling water until a loose dough forms. Knead the dough with floured hands for 1¹/₂–2 minutes or until smooth. Cover with plastic wrap and rest for 30 minutes. Break off walnut-sized pieces of dough and roll them out into thin ovals.

Fill a large frying pan with oil about ³/₄ inch high and heat over medium heat. When the oil is shimmering, cook the breads, two or three at a time, for 25–30 seconds each side or until crisp and golden. Drain on paper towels and serve warm.

Makes 40

Dal

1 cup red lentils, rinsed
1/4 teaspoon ground turmeric
1 tablespoon vegetable oil
1 tablespoon cumin seeds
1/2 teaspoon brown mustard seeds
1 onion, finely chopped
1 tablespoon grated, fresh ginger
2 long, fresh green chilies, seeded
  and finely chopped
1/3 cup lemon juice
2 tablespoons finely chopped cilantro
  leaves

Place the lentils in a saucepan with
3 cups cold water. Bring to a boil,
then reduce the heat and stir in the
turmeric. Simmer, covered, for
20 minutes or until tender.

Meanwhile, heat the oil in a saucepan
over medium heat and cook the
cumin and mustard seeds for
5–6 minutes or until the seeds begin
to pop. Add the onion, ginger, and
chilies, and cook for 5 minutes or until
the onion is golden. Add the lentils
and 1/2 cup water. Season with salt,
reduce the heat, and simmer for
10 minutes. Spoon into a bowl, stir
in the lemon juice, and garnish with
cilantro leaves.

Makes 3 cups

Cheese crackers

1 cup all-purpose flour
2 tablespoons self-rising flour
1 teaspoon curry powder
1/2 cup butter
1/2 cup grated Parmesan
2/3 cup grated cheddar
1 tablespoon crumbled, blue-vein
   cheese
1 tablespoon lemon juice
1/4 cup finely grated Parmesan, extra

Place the flours, curry powder, and butter in a food processor. Process until the mixture resembles fine breadcrumbs.

Stir in the cheeses and the lemon juice. Bring the mixture together into a ball.

Roll into a 12-inch log. Wrap in plastic wrap and chill for 1 hour. Slice into 1/4-inch slices. Reshape if necessary. Preheat the oven to 400°F.

Place on a baking parchment–lined baking sheet, allowing some room for spreading. Sprinkle the tops with Parmesan. Bake for 15 minutes or until the crackers are golden. Cool on the baking sheets.

Makes about 40

Cold

Buckwheat blini with smoked salmon

1/4-oz. packet active dry yeast
pinch of sugar
1 cup warm milk
3/4 cup buckwheat flour
1/2 cup all-purpose flour
2 eggs, separated
1 tablespoon butter
1/3 cup vegetable oil
2/3 cup crème fraîche
10 oz. smoked salmon, cut into
   3/4-inch strips
1 3/4 oz. salmon roe
fresh dill sprigs, to garnish

Place the yeast and sugar in a small bowl and gradually stir in the milk. Sift the flours into a large bowl and make a hollow in the center. Add the egg yolks and warm milk mixture and whisk until combined and smooth. Cover and allow to rest in a warm place for 45 minutes to rise.

Melt the butter, then stir into the risen dough and season. Place the egg whites in a clean, dry bowl and beat with an electric mixer until soft peaks form. Fold one third of the egg whites into the batter until just mixed. Gently fold in the remaining egg whites until just combined.

Heat 1 tablespoon of the oil in a large frying pan over medium heat. Drop 1/2 tablespoon of batter into the pan for each blini. Cook for 1 minute or until bubbles form on the surface. Turn over and cook for 30 seconds or until golden. Repeat to make about 40 blini, adding more oil as needed. Cool completely.

Spread 1 teaspoon of crème fraîche on each blini, then arrange a strip of smoked salmon over it. Spoon 1/4 teaspoon of salmon roe on top. Garnish with a sprig of dill and serve.

Makes about 40

Cucumber cups with Thai beef salad

4 small cucumbers
vegetable oil, for frying
8-oz. fillet of beef
1/2 red onion, finely chopped
20 fresh mint leaves, finely chopped
1 tablespoon finely chopped cilantro
  leaves
1 1/2 tablespoons fish sauce
1 1/2 tablespoons lime juice
1 fresh bird's-eye chili, seeded and
  finely chopped
1 teaspoon light brown sugar
small cilantro leaves, to garnish

Trim each end of the cucumbers but do not peel them. Cut each cucumber into 3/4-inch-thick slices; you should have twenty-four pieces. Scoop out the center of each slice with a melon baller, leaving a shell of flesh.

Heat a large frying pan over high heat and brush lightly with oil. Season the beef with salt and pepper, then place in the pan and cook for 1 1/2–2 minutes each side, depending on the thickness (the beef needs to be rare). Set aside to rest for 5 minutes. Thinly slice the beef across the grain, then slice each piece into 1/4-inch-wide strips and transfer to a bowl.

Add the onion, mint, and cilantro to the bowl and mix well. Combine the fish sauce, lime juice, chili, and sugar, stirring until the sugar has dissolved. Pour over the beef mixture and mix well. Fill each cucumber cup with the Thai beef salad and garnish with a whole cilantro leaf.

Makes 24

Think ahead: The cups can be prepared a day early. To store them, cover the surface with plastic wrap to keep them from drying out. Store in an airtight container. The meat can also be cooked a day early, but do not slice it until you are ready to assemble the salad.

Vegetable shapes with crème fraîche and fried leeks

2 ¾-lb. long, thin orange sweet
 potatoes, peeled
5 beets
½ cup crème fraîche
1 clove garlic, crushed
¼ teaspoon finely grated lime zest
vegetable oil, for deep-frying
2 leeks, cut into thin, 2-inch strips

Put the orange sweet potatoes in one large saucepan of water and put the beets in another. Bring them to a boil over high heat and simmer, covered, for 30–40 minutes or until tender, adding more boiling water if it starts to evaporate. Drain separately and set aside until cool enough to handle. Remove the skins from the beets. Trim the ends from the beets and sweet potatoes and cut both into ½-inch slices. Using a cookie cutter, cut the thin slices into shapes. Allow to drain on paper towels.

Place the crème fraîche, garlic, and lime zest in a bowl and mix together well. Refrigerate until ready to use.

Fill a deep, heavy-bottomed pan or deep-fryer one-third full of oil and heat to 375°F or until a cube of bread dropped into the oil browns in 10 seconds. Cook the leeks in four batches for 30 seconds or until lightly golden and crisp. Drain on crumpled paper towels and season to taste with some salt.

To assemble, place a teaspoon of the crème fraîche mixture on top of each vegetable shape and top with some fried leek strips.

Makes 35

Shrimp sushi cones

1½ cups sushi rice or short-grain rice
2 tablespoons seasoned rice vinegar
1 avocado
1 small cucumber
8 sheets nori, cut in half diagonally
1 teaspoon wasabi paste
½ cup pickled ginger
16 cooked medium shrimp, peeled
 and deveined
soy sauce, to serve

Place the rice in a strainer and rinse under cold running water. Set aside to drain for 1 hour. Place the drained rice in a large saucepan and add 1½ cups water. Cover and bring to a boil, then reduce the heat to very low and cook, tightly covered, for 15 minutes. Remove from the heat and leave the lid on for 10 minutes.

Transfer the rice to a large, shallow bowl and drizzle with the vinegar. Fold the vinegar through the rice, tossing lightly with a large metal spoon or spatula to cool as you combine. Do not use a stirring action; it will make the rice mushy.

Quarter and peel the avocado and cut each quarter into four long wedges. Trim the ends of the cucumber, then cut lengthwise into sixteen strips.

Hold a sheet of nori shiny-side down, flat in your hand. Place 2 tablespoons of rice on the left-hand side and spread out over half the nori sheet. Dab with a little wasabi and top with some pickled ginger. Place a strip each of avocado and cucumber on the rice and top with one shrimp. Roll up the nori to form a cone, enclosing the smaller end. Repeat, using all the ingredients. Serve with soy sauce.

Makes 16

Cherry tomato and bocconcini tartlets

2 cups all-purpose flour
1/2 cup chilled butter, chopped
1 egg

Filling
3/4 lb. cherry tomatoes, quartered
2 tablespoons olive oil
1 clove garlic, crushed
1 1/2 cups bocconcini, quartered
1/2 cup chopped Kalamata olives
1 tablespoon extra-virgin olive oil
1 tablespoon torn, fresh basil
vegetable oil, for deep-frying
30 small, fresh basil leaves

Preheat the oven to 400°F. Grease thirty small muffin cups. Sift the flour and rub the butter in with your fingers until the mixture resembles fine breadcrumbs. Make a well, add the egg, and mix with a spatula, using a cutting action, until beads form. Add a little cold water if needed. Press the dough into a ball, wrap in plastic wrap, and chill for 30 minutes.

Roll out the dough between two sheets of baking parchment to 1/8 inch thick. Cut thirty rounds with a 2 1/2-inch cutter and press a round into each muffin cup. Prick each bottom with a fork and bake for 6 minutes or until dry and golden. If they puff up, use a clean dishcloth to press back. Allow to cool.

To make the filling, preheat the oven to 400°F. Combine the tomatoes, olive oil, and garlic in a roasting pan and bake for 15 minutes or until golden. Cool, add the bocconcini, olives, extra-virgin olive oil, and basil, season, and toss. Fill a saucepan one-third full of oil and heat to 350°F or until a cube of bread browns in 15 seconds. Deep-fry the basil in batches for 30 seconds or until crisp. Drain. Spoon the vegetable mixture into the pastry cases and top with a basil leaf.

Makes 30

Dolmades

6½-oz. jar grape leaves in brine
1 cup medium-grain rice
1 small onion, finely chopped
1 tablespoon olive oil
⅓ cup pine nuts, toasted
2 tablespoons raisins
2 tablespoons chopped, fresh dill
2 tablespoons finely chopped,
   fresh mint
2 tablespoons finely chopped, fresh
   Italian parsley
⅓ cup olive oil, extra
2 tablespoons lemon juice
2 cups chicken or vegetable stock

Cover the grape leaves with cold water and soak for 15 minutes. Pat dry and cut off any stems. Set aside 5–6 leaves; discard any with holes. Pour boiling water over the rice and soak for 10 minutes, then drain.

Place the rice, onion, oil, pine nuts, raisins, herbs, and salt and pepper in a large bowl and mix well.

Lay some leaves vein-side down on a flat surface. Place ½ tablespoon of filling in the middle of each leaf, fold the stem end over the filling, then the left and right sides into the middle, and finally roll firmly towards the tip. It should resemble a fat cigar. Repeat to make forty-eight dolmades.

Line the bottom of a large, heavy-bottomed saucepan or flameproof casserole with the reserved leaves. Drizzle with 1 tablespoon of the extra oil. Put the dolmades in the saucepan, packing them tightly in one layer. Pour in the remaining oil and lemon juice.

Pour the stock over the dolmades and cover with an inverted plate to keep them from moving while cooking. Bring to a boil, then reduce the heat and simmer gently, covered, for 45 minutes. Remove with a slotted spoon. Serve warm or cold.

Makes 48

Oysters with lemon herb dressing

24 fresh oysters (see Notes)
1 tablespoon chopped, fresh dill
1 clove garlic, crushed
1 tablespoon finely chopped, fresh
  Italian parsley
2 teaspoons finely chopped, fresh
  chives
2 tablespoons lemon juice
1/4 cup extra-virgin olive oil
chive bows, to garnish
wheat bread, cubed, to garnish

Remove the oysters from the shells and pat dry. Wash the shells, replace the oysters, and cover with a damp cloth in the refrigerator.

Place the dill, garlic, parsley, chives, lemon juice, and oil in a bowl and season to taste with salt and cracked black pepper. Mix together well, then drizzle a little of the dressing over each oyster.

Garnish with chive bows and serve with tiny cubes of wheat bread.

Makes 24

Notes: Oysters are sold freshly shucked on the half shell, or alive and unshucked. When buying freshly shucked oysters, look for a plump, moist oyster. The flesh should be creamy with a clear liquid surrounding it. Oysters should smell like the fresh sea and have no traces of shell particles.

If you prefer to shuck them yourself, look for tightly closed, unbroken shells.

Oysters are often served on a bed of rock salt or crushed ice to help them remain stable and upright, and to keep them cool in summer.

Mandarin and duck rice paper rolls

1 whole Chinese roast duck
24 small Vietnamese rice paper
   wrappers
3 mandarin oranges, peeled and
   segmented
1 cup fresh mint
12 fresh chives, cut into 1 1/2-inch
   pieces
2 tablespoons hoisin sauce
2 tablespoons fresh mandarin orange
   juice

Remove the flesh and skin from the duck and shred into 1/2 x 1 1/4-inch pieces.

Working with one wrapper at a time, briefly soak each wrapper in cold water until softened, then place on a dry dishcloth. Arrange 2 or 3 pieces of duck at the end of the wrapper closest to you. Top with 2 segments of orange, 3 mint leaves, and several chive pieces. Fold the end closest to you over the filling, fold in the sides, and firmly roll up the rice paper to form a small spring roll.

Combine the hoisin sauce and mandarin juice in a bowl and serve as a dipping sauce with the rice paper rolls. These are best served immediately, as the rolls will start to dry out if left for too long.

Makes 24

Rolled omelette with ocean trout caviar

4 eggs
$1/3$ cup heavy whipping cream
4 tablespoons finely chopped, fresh
  chives
1 tablespoon olive oil
2 tablespoons butter, melted
3 slices white bread
$1/4$ cup sour cream
4 oz. salmon roe
chopped, fresh chives, to garnish

Whisk together an egg, 1 tablespoon of the cream, and 1 tablespoon of the chopped chives, and season with salt and cracked black pepper. Pour into a 10-inch, lightly greased, nonstick frying pan and cook over medium heat on one side for 3 minutes or until just set. The omelettes will be difficult to roll if overcooked. Turn out onto a sheet of baking parchment. Repeat until you have four omelettes.

Tightly roll one omelette into a neat roll, then take another omelette and wrap it around the first. Repeat with the remaining omelettes so that you have two rolls. Wrap separately in plastic wrap and refrigerate for 1 hour.

Meanwhile, preheat the oven to 350°F. Combine the oil and butter. Using a 1$1/4$-inch cutter, cut twenty-four rounds from the bread and brush with the butter and oil mixture. Place on a baking sheet and bake for 20–30 minutes or until crisp and golden. Allow to cool.

Cut each of the cooled omelette rolls into twelve rounds. Spread $1/2$ teaspoon of the sour cream onto each crouton, and put a round of omelette on top. Top with a teaspoon of salmon roe and garnish with chopped chives.

Makes 24

Chicken liver parfait

2 tablespoons butter
2 shallots, peeled and sliced
1 lb. chicken livers, any fat removed
1/4 cup heavy whipping cream
1 tablespoon cognac or brandy
48 melba toasts
8 cornichons (baby gherkins), thinly
  sliced diagonally

Heat a large frying pan over medium heat. Melt the butter, then add the shallots to the pan and cook, stirring, for 4–5 minutes or until they are soft and transparent. Use a slotted spoon to transfer them to a food processor.

In the same pan, add the chicken livers and cook in batches over high heat, stirring, for 4–5 minutes or until seared on the outside but still pink and quite soft on the inside. Add to the food processor, along with 2 tablespoons of the pan juices, the cream, cognac, and some salt and pepper. Blend for 4–5 minutes or until quite smooth. Push through a fine strainer to remove any lumps. Transfer to a bowl or serving dish, put plastic wrap directly on the surface of the mixture, and refrigerate for at least 4 hours or until cold.

To serve, spoon a heaping teaspoon of parfait onto each melba toast and top with a slice of cornichon. Alternatively, leave the parfait in the serving dish, supply a small knife, and allow guests to help themselves.

Makes 48

Think ahead: The parfait can be made up to three days in advance and stored in the refrigerator in an airtight container. Assemble no more than 30 minutes before serving.

Quail eggs with spiced salts

2 teaspoons cumin seeds
48 quail eggs
1/2 cup salt
1 1/2 teaspoons Chinese five-spice
   powder
3 teaspoons celery salt

Dry-fry the cumin seeds over low heat for 1–2 minutes or until fragrant. Cool slightly, then grind until finely crushed into a powder.

Place half the eggs in a large saucepan of water, bring to a boil, and cook for 1 1/2 minutes for medium-hard boiled eggs. Remove from the saucepan and rinse under cold water to cool. Repeat with the remaining eggs. Peel when cold—this is more easily done under gently running, cold water.

Divide the salt among three small bowls and add the Chinese five-spice powder to one, the celery salt to another, and the ground cumin to the third. Mix the flavorings into the salt in each bowl.

To serve, pile the eggs into a large bowl and serve each of the salts in a small bowl. Invite your guests to dip their egg into the flavored salt of their choice.

Makes 48

Think ahead: The eggs can be prepared the day before they are to be served and the spiced salts can be made up to 2 weeks earlier and stored in airtight containers.

Asparagus and prosciutto with hollandaise sauce

24 fresh asparagus spears, trimmed
8 slices prosciutto, cut into thirds
  lengthwise

Hollandaise sauce
3/4 cup butter
4 egg yolks
1 tablespoon lemon juice
ground white pepper

Blanch the asparagus in boiling, salted water for 2 minutes, then drain and rinse in cold water. Pat dry, then cut the spears in half. Lay the bottom half of each spear next to its tip, then secure together by wrapping a piece of prosciutto around them.

To make the hollandaise sauce, melt the butter in a saucepan. Skim any froth off the top. Cool the butter a little. Combine the egg yolks and 2 tablespoons of water in a heatproof bowl placed over a saucepan of simmering water, making sure the bottom of the bowl does not touch the water. Using a wire whisk, beat for 3–4 minutes or until the mixture is thick and foamy. Make sure the bowl does not get too hot or the eggs will scramble. Add the butter slowly at first, whisking well between each addition. Keep adding the butter in a thin stream, whisking continuously, until all the butter has been used. Try to avoid using the milky whey in the bottom of the saucepan. Stir in the lemon juice and season with salt and white pepper. Place in a bowl and serve warm with the asparagus.

Makes 24 bundles

Vegetable frittata with hummus and black olives

2 large red peppers
1¼ lbs. orange sweet potatoes, cut into ½-inch slices
¼ cup olive oil
2 leeks, finely sliced
2 cloves garlic, crushed
½ lb. zucchini, thinly sliced
1 lb. eggplants, cut into ½-inch slices
8 eggs, lightly beaten
2 tablespoons finely chopped, fresh basil
1¼ cups grated Parmesan
1 cup hummus
black olives, pitted and halved, to garnish

Cut the peppers into large pieces, removing the seeds and membrane. Place, skin-side up, under a hot broiler until the skin blackens and blisters. Cool in a plastic bag, then peel.

Boil the sweet potatoes for 5 minutes or until just tender. Drain.

Heat 1 tablespoon of the oil in a deep, 9-inch frying pan over medium heat. Stir in the leeks and garlic for 1 minute or until soft. Add the zucchini and cook for 2 minutes, then remove.

Heat the remaining oil in the same pan and cook the eggplant slices in batches for 2 minutes each side or until golden. Line the bottom of the pan with half the eggplant slices and spread with the leek mixture. Cover with the roasted peppers, then with the remaining eggplant slices, and finally the sweet potatoes.

Mix the eggs, basil, Parmesan, and pepper in a bowl. Pour over the vegetables. Cook over low heat for 15 minutes or until almost cooked. Place the saucepan under a hot broiler for 2–3 minutes or until golden and cooked. Cool before inverting onto a board. Trim the edges and cut into thirty squares. Top each square with some hummus and half an olive.

Makes 30 pieces

Smoked trout sandwiches

24 slices wheat bread
softened cream cheese, to spread
1 large cucumber, cut into
   wafer-thin slices
3/4 lb. smoked trout
2 tablespoons roughly chopped,
   fresh dill
lemon wedges, to garnish

Spread the bread with cream cheese.
Arrange a single layer of cucumber
on half the bread slices. Layer the
trout on top of the cucumber, then
place the other bread slices on top.
Cut off the crusts, then slice each
sandwich into four triangles.

Place the sandwiches, long-edge
down, on a platter to form a pyramid.
Brush one side of the pyramid with
softened cream cheese, then sprinkle
with dill. Garnish with lemon.

Makes 48

Mexican bites

24-oz. can kidney beans, drained
1 teaspoon ground cumin
2 tablespoons olive oil
1/4 teaspoon cayenne pepper
1 avocado
1 small clove garlic, crushed
2 tablespoons sour cream
2 tablespoons lime juice
1 vine-ripened tomato, seeded and
  finely chopped
2 tablespoons finely chopped cilantro
8-oz. bag round tortilla chips

To make refried beans, put the kidney beans in a bowl and mash well with a potato masher, then add the cumin. Heat 1 1/2 tablespoons of oil in a large, nonstick frying pan and add the cayenne pepper and mashed kidney beans. Cook over medium-high heat for 2–3 minutes, stirring constantly. Allow to cool, then refrigerate for 30 minutes or until cold.

To make guacamole, scoop the avocado flesh into a food processor and add the garlic, sour cream, and 1 tablespoon of the lime juice. Process for a few minutes until it is a thick, creamy paste, then add salt to taste. Refrigerate.

To make the salsa, mix together the tomato, cilantro, and the remaining olive oil and lime juice in a bowl. Refrigerate until needed.

To assemble, lay out thirty-six round tortilla chips. Put a heaping teaspoon of refried beans in the center of each chip, add a teaspoon of the guacamole, and then half a teaspoon of salsa.

Makes 36

Think ahead: The bean puree can be made three days in advance. Make the salsa up to 2 hours beforehand. Assemble just before serving.

Vietnamese shrimp rolls

²/₃ cup lime juice
2 teaspoons grated lime zest
¹/₃ cup sweet chili sauce
2 teaspoons fish sauce
2 teaspoons light brown sugar
5 6-inch rice paper wrappers
12 cooked medium shrimp, peeled
  and halved lengthwise
1 small carrot, cut into 2-inch strips
1 small cucumber, cut into 2-inch
  strips
¹/₂ avocado, sliced
3 tablespoons cilantro leaves
2 tablespoons torn, fresh mint
  (Vietnamese, if available)
5 scallions, thinly sliced diagonally

Combine the lime juice, zest, sweet
chili sauce, fish sauce, and sugar in
a small bowl.

Working with one rice paper wrapper
at a time, dip a wrapper in a bowl of
warm water for 10 seconds to soften,
then lay out on a flat surface. Place
two shrimp halves and a little of each
remaining ingredient at one end of the
wrapper, then drizzle with 1 teaspoon
of the sauce. Fold in the sides and roll
up tightly. Serve with the remaining
sauce for dipping.

Makes 12

Thai-style crab tartlets

2 cups all-purpose flour
1/2 cup chilled butter, chopped
1 egg

Filling
1/4 cup lime juice
1 tablespoon fish sauce
1 tablespoon light brown sugar
10 oz. fresh crabmeat, shredded
  and well drained
2 tablespoons chopped cilantro
  leaves
1 tablespoon chopped, fresh mint
  (Vietnamese, if available)
1 small, fresh red chili, finely chopped
2 kaffir lime leaves, finely shredded

Preheat the oven to 400°F. Lightly grease thirty small muffin cups. Sift the flour into a bowl and rub the butter in with your fingers until the mixture resembles fine breadcrumbs. Make a well in the center, add the egg, and mix with a rubber spatula or palette knife, using a cutting action, until it comes together in beads. If the dough seems too dry, add a little cold water. Press the dough into a ball on a lightly floured surface, then wrap it in plastic wrap and refrigerate for 30 minutes.

Roll out the dough between two sheets of baking parchment to 1/8 inch thick and cut out thirty rounds with a 2 1/2-inch cutter. Press a round into each muffin cup. Prick the bottoms with a fork and bake for 6–8 minutes or until golden. If they puff up, use a clean dishcloth to press out any air pockets. Cool.

Combine the lime juice, fish sauce, and sugar in a bowl and stir until the sugar is dissolved. Mix in the rest of the ingredients, then spoon into the prepared pastry cases and serve.

Makes 30

Plan ahead: The pastry cases can be made 2–3 days ahead and kept in an airtight container. Crisp them in a 325°F oven for 5 minutes.

Vietnamese rice paper rolls

Nuoc cham dipping sauce
3/4 cup fish sauce
1/4 cup lime juice
2 tablespoons light brown sugar
2 bird's-eye chilies, seeded and
   finely chopped

1/4 lb. dried rice vermicelli
48 6-inch, round rice paper wrappers
48 large shrimp, cooked, peeled,
   deveined, and halved lengthwise
1 2/3 cups bean sprouts
3 cups fresh mint
2 cups cilantro leaves

To make the dipping sauce, combine all the ingredients and 1/2 cup water and stir until the sugar dissolves. Transfer to two small serving dishes and set aside.

Place the noodles in a heatproof bowl, cover with boiling water, and soak for 10 minutes, then drain.

Assemble the rolls one at a time. Dip a rice paper wrapper in a bowl of warm water for 30 seconds or until it softens. Place the wrapper on a work surface and put 2 shrimp halves on the bottom third of the wrapper. Top with a few noodles, bean sprouts, 3 mint leaves, and 6 cilantro leaves, in that order. Ensure that the filling is neat and compact, then turn up the bottom of the wrapper to cover the filling. Holding the filling in place, fold in the two sides, then roll up.

Arrange on a platter, folded-side down. Cover with a damp dishcloth or plastic wrap until ready to serve. Serve with the dipping sauce.

Makes 48

Think ahead: You can make the rolls up to 8 hours beforehand, but make sure you cover them well or they will dry out rapidly. The sauce can be made a day early.

Smoked fish pâté with bruschetta

2 13-oz. smoked rainbow trout fillets,
  skin and bones removed
2–3 tablespoons lemon or lime juice
1/2 cup cream cheese, softened
3/4 cup butter, melted
sprigs of fresh herbs such as dill,
  fennel, or Italian parsley, to garnish
lemon slices, to garnish

Bruschetta
1 loaf French bread, sliced diagonally
  into 24 thin slices
1/3 cup olive oil
3 cloves garlic

Remove the skin and bones from
the fish and roughly flake the flesh.
Process the flesh in a blender or
food processor with the juice, cream
cheese, and melted butter until the
mixture is quite smooth. Season
to taste with ground black pepper.

Spoon into a 2-cup ramekin and
refrigerate overnight or until the
mixture has firmed. Keep refrigerated
until ready to serve. Garnish with
sprigs of fresh herbs and lemon slices.

For the bruschetta, preheat the oven
to 400°F. Brush both sides of the
bread slices lightly with oil, then
spread on a baking sheet and bake
for 10–15 minutes or until crisp and
golden, turning once. Remove from
the oven and rub all over one side
of each slice with a garlic clove,
using a clove for every eight slices.
Serve with the pâté.

Soybean terrine

1 cup dried soybeans
1 tablespoon soybean oil
1 onion, finely chopped
1 zucchini, grated
1/4 cup finely chopped, fresh
  Italian parsley
1 teaspoon cayenne pepper
3 eggs, lightly beaten
1/3 cup sour cream
1/4 cup lemon juice
2 cups grated cheddar
1/2 cup grated Parmesan
store-bought tomato relish, to serve

Soak the soybeans in a bowl with plenty of cold water for at least 8 hours or preferably overnight. Drain well. Place the soybeans in a large saucepan and add enough water to cover the beans. Bring to a boil, then simmer for 1 1/2 hours or until tender. Drain.

Preheat the oven to 375°F. Lightly grease a standard loaf pan and line the bottom and sides with baking parchment. Blend the beans in a food processor until crumbly.

Heat the oil in a large frying pan. Add the onion and zucchini and cook over medium heat for 5 minutes or until golden. Transfer to a bowl and allow to cool.

Add the parsley, cayenne pepper, eggs, sour cream, lemon juice, cheeses, and soybeans, and mix together. Spoon the mixture into the prepared pan and press down to flatten the top. Bake for 45 minutes or until firm. Cool completely in the pan, then carefully invert and unmold on a platter. Serve sliced, garnished with relish, tomatoes, and thyme.

Serves 6–8

Corn muffins

2½ cups self-rising flour
½ cup cornmeal
1 cup milk
½ cup butter, melted
2 eggs, lightly beaten
4½-oz. can corn, drained
2 scallions, finely chopped
½ cup grated cheddar

Preheat the oven to 415°F. Grease a 12-cup muffin pan with butter. Sift the flour and cornmeal into a large bowl and make a hollow in the center.

Whisk together the milk, butter, eggs, corn, scallions, cheddar, and salt and pepper in a separate bowl, and pour into the hollow. Fold gently with a metal spoon until all the ingredients are just combined. Do not overmix—the mixture should still be very lumpy.

Spoon the mixture into the pan and bake for 20–25 minutes or until lightly golden. Leave for 5 minutes before removing from the pan. Serve split in half spread with butter or cream cheese. Delicious warm or at room temperature.

Makes 12

Variation: Try adding 2 tablespoons chopped chives, ¼ cup chopped, drained, sun-dried tomatoes or peppers in oil, 2 finely chopped slices of bacon, 2 finely chopped red chilies or ½ finely chopped red or green pepper into the mixture with the milk and cheddar. Another delicious variation is to sprinkle sesame or sunflower seeds over the muffins just before baking.

Bloody Mary oyster shots

⅓ cup vodka
½ cup tomato juice
1 tablespoon lemon juice
dash of Worcestershire sauce
2 drops hot pepper sauce
pinch of celery salt
12 oysters
1 cucumber, peeled, seeded, and
  finely julienned

Combine the vodka, tomato juice, lemon juice, Worcestershire sauce, hot pepper sauce, and celery salt in a pitcher. Mix well, then refrigerate for 30 minutes or until chilled.

Just before serving, fill each shot glass about two-thirds full. Drop an oyster in each glass, then top with a teaspoon of cucumber. For the final touch, crack some black pepper over the top of each shot glass, then serve.

Serves 12

Note: It is better to use oysters fresh from the shell rather than from a jar because they have a much better, fresher taste.
Think ahead: The tomato mixture can be made a day ahead and kept in the refrigerator. Stir before serving.
Variation: If you think your guests are game enough for some fire in their evening, make chilled sake shots. Fill each glass two-thirds full of sake, add an oyster, then garnish with the cucumber.

Smoked salmon breadbaskets

8 oz. smoked salmon
1 loaf sliced white bread
1/4 cup olive oil
1/3 cup mayonnaise
2 teaspoons extra-virgin olive oil
1 teaspoon white wine vinegar
1 teaspoon finely chopped, fresh dill
3 teaspoons horseradish cream
3 tablespoons salmon roe
fresh dill sprigs, to garnish

Preheat the oven to 350°F. Cut the salmon into 3/4-inch-wide strips. Flatten the bread to 1/16 inch with a rolling pin, then cut out twenty-four rounds with a 2 3/4-inch cutter. Brush both sides of the rounds with oil and push into the cups of two 12-cup muffin pans. Bake for 10 minutes or until crisp. Allow to cool.

Stir the mayonnaise in a bowl with the extra-virgin olive oil, vinegar, dill, and horseradish until combined.

Arrange folds of salmon in each cooled breadbasket and top each with 1 teaspoon of mayonnaise mixture. Spoon 1/2 teaspoon of salmon roe on top of each, garnish with dill, and serve.

Makes 24

Note: The breadbaskets can be made a day in advance. When completely cold, store in an airtight container. If they soften, you can crisp them on a baking sheet in a 350°F oven for 5 minutes. Cool before filling.

Cold

Herbed griddle cakes with pear and blue cheese topping

1 cup self-rising flour
2 eggs, lightly beaten
1/2 cup milk
2 tablespoons finely chopped,
   fresh parsley
2 teaspoons finely chopped,
   fresh sage

Pear and blue cheese topping
2/3 cup Blue Castello or other creamy
   blue cheese
1/3 cup cream cheese
2 teaspoons brandy
1 large, ripe, green-skinned pear
1/4 cup toasted walnuts, finely
   chopped
1/2 lemon
1/2 bunch chives, cut into 1 1/2-inch
   pieces

Sift the flour into a bowl and make a hollow in the center. Gradually add the combined eggs and milk, mixing the flour in slowly. When the flour is incorporated, add the parsley and sage and season well. Whisk until a smooth batter forms.

Heat a large, nonstick frying pan over medium heat and spray with cooking oil spray. Drop heaping teaspoons of batter into the pan and flatten to 2-inch rounds. Cook until bubbles appear in the surface of the griddle cake, then turn and brown the other side. Remove and cool on a wire rack.

To make the topping, beat the cheeses and brandy together until smooth. Season with pepper. Cut the pear in half and peel and core one half. Dice it into 1/4-inch pieces, leaving the other half untouched. Stir the diced pear and walnuts into the cheese mixture. Core the other half of the pear but do not peel it. Thinly slice the pear lengthwise. Cut each slice into 3/4-inch triangles with green skin on one side. Squeeze some lemon juice over the cut surfaces to prevent discoloration.

Spread 1 teaspoon of topping on each griddle cake. Top with three pear triangles and garnish with chives.

Makes 36

174

Mini frittatas

2 lbs. orange sweet potatoes
1 tablespoon vegetable oil
2 tablespoons butter
4 leeks, white part only, finely sliced
2 cloves garlic, crushed
1²/₃ cups feta, crumbled
8 eggs
½ cup whipping cream

Preheat the oven to 350°F. Grease or brush two 6-cup muffin pans with oil or melted butter. Cut small rounds of baking parchment and place into the bottom of each cup. Cut the sweet potatoes into small cubes and boil, steam, or microwave until tender. Drain well and set aside.

Heat the oil and butter in a frying pan and cook the leeks for 10 minutes, stirring occasionally, or until very soft and lightly golden. Add the garlic and cook for another minute. Cool, then stir in the feta and sweet potatoes. Divide the mixture evenly among the muffin cups.

Whisk the eggs and cream together and season with salt and cracked black pepper. Pour the egg mixture into each cup until three-quarters filled, then press the vegetables down gently. Bake for 25–30 minutes or until golden and set. Leave in the pans for 5 minutes, then ease out with a knife and cool on a wire rack.

Makes 12

Thai beef salad rice paper rolls

Dipping sauce
¼ cup Japanese soy sauce
1 tablespoon rice vinegar
1 teaspoon sesame oil
1 tablespoon mirin
2 teaspoons finely julienned, fresh ginger

⅓ cup kecap manis
⅓ cup lime juice
1 tablespoon sesame oil
2 small, fresh red chilies, finely chopped
10 oz. rib-eye steak
1 lemongrass stalk, white part only, finely chopped
¼ cup lime juice, extra
3 tablespoons finely chopped, fresh mint
3 tablespoons finely chopped cilantro leaves
1½ tablespoons fish sauce
16 6½-inch-square rice paper wrappers

To make the dipping sauce, place the Japanese soy sauce, rice vinegar, sesame oil, mirin, and ginger in a small bowl and mix together well.

Mix the kecap manis, lime juice, sesame oil, and half the chopped chilies in a large bowl. Add the beef and toss well to ensure that all the beef is coated. Cover with plastic wrap and refrigerate for 2 hours.

Heat a ridged grill pan over high heat and cook the beef for 2–3 minutes each side or until cooked to your liking. Cool, then slice against the grain into thin strips.

Combine the beef in a nonmetallic bowl with the lemongrass, extra lime juice, mint, cilantro, fish sauce, and remaining chili pieces, then toss well.

Dip each rice paper wrapper in warm water for a few seconds until soft. Drain, then place a tablespoon of the mixture in the center of the rice paper wrapper and roll up, tucking in the edges. Repeat with the remaining ingredients to make sixteen rolls. Serve with the dipping sauce.

Makes 16

Maki sushi

1 1/4 cups sushi rice
1/4 cup rice vinegar
1 tablespoon sugar
1/2 tablespoon mirin

8 oz. sashimi tuna or imitation crab
  sticks
1 small cucumber
1/2 avocado
8 sheets nori
3 teaspoons wasabi paste

Rinse the rice under running water until the water runs clear, then drain thoroughly. Place in a large saucepan with 1 1/2 cups water and simmer for 20–25 minutes or until tender. Cover with a clean dishcloth and leave for 15 minutes.

Combine the vinegar, sugar, mirin, and 1 teaspoon salt, and stir until the sugar dissolves. Spread the rice over a shallow, nonmetallic container and pour the dressing on top. Mix with a spatula, separating the grains of rice. Allow to cool to room temperature.

Cut the tuna, cucumber, and avocado into thin strips. Place a sheet of nori on a bamboo mat (sold in Asian markets), shiny-side down, with a short end toward you. Spread the rice 1/2 inch thick over the nori, leaving a 1/2-inch border. Make a shallow groove down the center of the rice toward the short end closest to you. Spread some wasabi along the groove. Place a selection of strips of your filling ingredients on top of the wasabi. Lift the edge of the bamboo mat and roll the sushi, starting from the edge nearest to you. When you've finished rolling, press the mat to make either a round or square roll. Wet a sharp knife, trim the ends, and cut the roll into six pieces.

Makes 48

Wild mushroom pâté on melba toasts

¾ oz. dried wild mushrooms (e.g.,
  porcini, chanterelles, morels)
¼ cup butter
¾ lb. portobello mushrooms, sliced
1 garlic clove, crushed
2 tablespoons brandy
¼ cup heavy whipping cream
1 teaspoon fresh thyme
¼ teaspoon juniper berries, ground
30 mini melba toasts
crème fraîche, to serve
30 fresh Italian parsley leaves

Soak the dried mushrooms in a bowl with 1 cup hot (not boiling) water for 2 hours or until soft. Drain, saving 2 tablespoons of the soaking liquid. Discard any pieces of mushroom that are still tough and woody after soaking.

Melt the butter in a large frying pan over medium heat, then add the mushrooms and sauté for 5 minutes. Add the garlic and cook for 1 minute, then add the dried mushrooms and soaking liquid and cook for another 5–8 minutes, stirring regularly. Pour in the brandy and cook for 2 minutes or until evaporated. Remove from the heat and allow to cool for 10 minutes.

Transfer the cooled mushroom mixture to a food processor with the cream, thyme, ground juniper berries, and ½ teaspoon each of salt and cracked black pepper and blend for 4–5 minutes or until finely chopped.

Spoon the pâté into a bowl and refrigerate, covered, for at least 3 hours or until chilled. Put a teaspoon of pâté on each toast and top with ½ teaspoon crème fraîche and a fresh parsley leaf.

Makes 30

Hot

Steamed shrimp nori rolls

1 lb. shrimp, peeled and deveined
1 1/2 tablespoons fish sauce
1 tablespoon sake
2 tablespoons chopped cilantro
1 large, fresh kaffir lime leaf, finely
    shredded
1 tablespoon lime juice
2 teaspoons sweet chili sauce
1 egg white, lightly beaten
5 sheets nori

Dipping sauce
1/4 cup sake
1/4 cup soy sauce
1 tablespoon mirin
1 tablespoon lime juice

Process the shrimp in a food processor or blender with the fish sauce, sake, cilantro, kaffir lime leaf, lime juice, and sweet chili sauce until smooth. Add the egg white and pulse for a few seconds until just combined.

Lay the nori sheets on a flat surface and spread some shrimp mixture over each sheet, leaving a 3/4-inch border at one end. Roll up tightly, cover, and refrigerate for 1 hour or until firm. Using a very sharp knife, trim the ends, then cut into 3/4-inch pieces.

Place the rolls in a lined bamboo steamer. Cover the steamer and place it over a wok of simmering water, making sure it doesn't touch the water. Steam for 5 minutes or until heated thoroughly.

For the dipping sauce, thoroughly mix all the ingredients together in a small bowl. Serve with the nori rolls.

Makes 25

Chicken san choy bau

1½ tablespoons vegetable oil
¼ teaspoon sesame oil
3 cloves garlic, crushed
3 teaspoons grated, fresh ginger
6 scallions, thinly sliced
1 lb. ground chicken
⅓ cup drained water chestnuts,
    finely chopped
⅓ cup drained bamboo shoots,
    finely chopped
¼ cup oyster sauce
2 teaspoons soy sauce
¼ cup sherry
1 teaspoon sugar
4 small Belgian endive heads,
    bottoms trimmed
oyster sauce, to serve

Heat the oils in a wok or large frying pan, add the garlic, ginger, and half the scallions, and stir-fry over high heat for 1 minute. Add the ground chicken and continue cooking for 3–4 minutes or until just cooked, breaking up any lumps with a fork.

Add the water chestnuts, bamboo shoots, oyster and soy sauces, sherry, sugar, and the remaining scallions. Cook for 2–3 minutes or until the liquid thickens a little.

Allow the mixture to cool slightly before dividing among the Belgian endive leaves—you will need about 2 heaping teaspoons per leaf. Drizzle with oyster sauce and serve.

Makes about 36

Think ahead: The filling can be made up to 2 days in advance and reheated just before assembling.
Variations: Ground pork is another popular choice for san choy bau. You can either substitute it directly for the ground chicken or use half of each and mix them together. Several types of leaves work well for holding the filling. Try the small leaves from romaine or iceberg lettuce, or for a more sophisticated option, try betel leaves.

Bell pepper muffins with tapenade and mascarpone

1 red pepper, cut into large, flattish pieces
2 cups all-purpose flour
3 teaspoons baking powder
3/4 cup grated Parmesan
1/2 cup milk
2 eggs, lightly beaten
1/4 cup olive oil
1 1/2 tablespoons olive oil, extra
24 fresh basil leaves
1/3 cup mascarpone

Tapenade
1/2 cup pitted Kalamata olives
1 clove garlic, chopped
2 anchovies (optional)
2 teaspoons drained capers
2 tablespoons olive oil
2 teaspoons lemon juice

Cook the pepper, skin-side up, under a hot broiler until the skin blisters. Allow to cool in a plastic bag. Peel the skin and finely chop the flesh.

Preheat the oven to 350°F. Grease two nonstick, 12-cup muffin pans. Sift the flour and baking powder, add the pepper and Parmesan, and season. Make a hollow. Fold in the combined milk, eggs, and oil with a spoon. Do not overmix—it should be lumpy.

Fill each muffin cup with the mixture. Bake for 15–20 minutes or until a skewer comes out clean. Cool slightly, then lift out onto a wire rack.

Meanwhile, to make the tapenade, blend the olives, garlic, anchovies, and capers in a food processor until finely chopped. Then, while the motor is running, add the oil and lemon juice to form a paste. Season with pepper.

Heat the extra oil in a saucepan and fry the basil leaves until they are crisp. Remove and drain on paper towels.

While still warm, cut the tops off the muffins. Spread 1/2 teaspoon of mascarpone on each muffin, then add 1/2 teaspoon of tapenade. Top with a basil leaf before replacing the tops.

Makes 24

Crumbed shrimp with ponzu dipping sauce

18 jumbo shrimp
2 tablespoons cornstarch
3 eggs
3 cups fresh breadcrumbs
vegetable oil, for frying
$\frac{1}{3}$ cup ponzu sauce or $\frac{1}{4}$ cup soy
   sauce combined with 1 tablespoon
   lemon juice

Peel and devein the shrimp, leaving the tails intact. Cut down the back of each shrimp to form a butterfly. Place each shrimp between two layers of plastic wrap and gently beat to form a cutlet.

Put the cornstarch, eggs, and breadcrumbs in separate bowls. Lightly beat the eggs. Dip each shrimp first into the cornstarch, then into the egg, and finally into the breadcrumbs, ensuring that each cutlet is well covered in crumbs.

Heat the oil in a frying pan over medium heat until hot. Cook six shrimp cutlets at a time for 1 minute each side or until the crumbs are golden—be careful they don't burn. Serve immediately with ponzu sauce.

Makes 18

Note: Ponzu is a Japanese dipping sauce usually used for sashimi.

Falafel

2 cups dried chickpeas
  (garbanzo beans)
1 onion, finely chopped
2 cloves garlic, crushed
2 tablespoons chopped, fresh parsley
1 tablespoon chopped cilantro
2 teaspoons ground cumin
$1/2$ teaspoon baking powder
vegetable oil, for deep-frying

Soak the chickpeas in 3 cups of water for 4 hours or overnight. Drain and place in a food processor, then process for 30 seconds or until the chickpeas are finely ground.

Add the onion, garlic, parsley, cilantro, cumin, baking powder, 1 tablespoon of water, salt and pepper, and process for 10 seconds or until the mixture forms a rough paste. Cover and leave for 30 minutes.

Using your hands, shape heaping tablespoons of the falafel mixture into balls and squeeze out any excess liquid. Heat a deep, heavy-bottomed pan one-third full of oil to 350°F or until a cube of bread browns in 15 seconds. Gently lower the falafel balls into the oil. Cook in batches of five, for 3–4 minutes each batch. When the balls are browned, remove with a large slotted spoon. Drain well. Serve with Lebanese or pita bread, tabbouleh, and hummus.

Makes 30

Spiced carrot soup shot

1/3 cup olive oil

2 teaspoons honey

3 teaspoons ground cumin

3 teaspoons coriander seeds, lightly crushed

2 cinnamon sticks, broken in half

3 lbs. carrots, cut into 1 1/4-inch chunks

3 cups chicken stock

1/3 cup whipping cream

3/4 cup sour cream

3 tablespoons cilantro leaves

Preheat the oven to 400°F. Combine the oil, honey, cumin, coriander seeds, cinnamon sticks, 1 teaspoon salt, and plenty of cracked black pepper in a roasting pan. Add the chunks of carrot and mix well to ensure that the carrots are entirely coated in the spice mixture.

Roast for 1 hour or until the carrots are tender, shaking the pan occasionally during cooking. Remove from the oven, discard the cinnamon sticks with tongs, and allow the carrots to cool slightly.

Transfer half the carrot chunks, 1 1/2 cups of the stock, and a cup of water to a food processor or blender and blend until smooth. Strain through a fine strainer into a clean saucepan. Repeat with the remaining carrots, stock, and another 1 cup water. Bring the soup to a simmer and cook for 10 minutes. Add the whipping cream and season to taste. Pour into shot glasses or espresso cups. Garnish each cup with 1/4 teaspoon sour cream and a cilantro leaf.

Serves 36 (Makes 6 cups)

Think ahead: The soup can be refrigerated for 2 days or frozen for up to 8 weeks, before the whipping cream is added.

Pork and noodle balls with sweet chili sauce

Dipping sauce
1/3 cup sweet chili sauce
2 teaspoons mirin
2 teaspoons finely chopped, fresh
   ginger
1/2 cup Japanese soy sauce

8 oz. Hokkien noodles
10 oz. ground pork
6 scallions, finely chopped
2 cloves garlic, crushed
1/3 cup finely chopped cilantro leaves
1 tablespoon fish sauce
2 tablespoons oyster sauce
1 1/2 tablespoons lime juice
peanut oil, for deep-frying

To make the dipping sauce, combine the sweet chili sauce, mirin, ginger, and Japanese soy sauce in a bowl.

Place the noodles in a bowl and cover with boiling water. Soak for 1 minute or until tender. Drain well and pat dry with paper towels. Cut the noodles into 2-inch pieces, then transfer to a large bowl. Add the ground pork, scallions, garlic, cilantro leaves, fish sauce, oyster sauce, and lime juice, and combine the mixture well with your hands, making sure the pork is evenly distributed throughout the noodles.

Roll tablespoons of mixture into balls, making 30 in total. Press each ball firmly to ensure it sticks together during cooking.

Fill a wok or large saucepan a third full of oil and heat to 325°F or until a cube of bread browns in 20 seconds. Deep-fry the pork balls in batches for 2–3 minutes or until golden and cooked through. Drain on paper towels. Serve hot with the dipping sauce.

Makes 30

Storage: The dipping sauce is best made up to a week in advance to allow the flavors to infuse.

Stuffed black olives

36 pitted, jumbo black or large
   Kalamata olives
3½ oz. goat cheese
1 teaspoon capers, drained and finely
   chopped
1 clove garlic, crushed
1 tablespoon chopped, fresh Italian
   parsley

1½ tablespoons all-purpose flour
2 eggs, lightly beaten
1 cup dry breadcrumbs
1 tablespoon finely chopped, fresh
   Italian parsley, extra
vegetable oil, for deep-frying

Carefully cut the olives along the open cavity so they are opened out, but still in one piece.

Mash the goat cheese, capers, garlic, and parsley together in a small bowl, then season. Push an even amount of the mixture into the cavity of the olives, then press them closed.

Put the flour in one small bowl, the egg in another, and combine the breadcrumbs and extra parsley in a third bowl. Dip each olive first into the flour, then into the egg, and finally into the breadcrumbs. Put the crumbed olives on a plate and refrigerate for at least 2 hours.

Fill a deep, heavy-bottomed pan or deep-fryer one-third full of oil and heat to 350°F or until a cube of bread dropped into the oil browns in 15 seconds. Cook the olives in batches for 1–2 minutes or until golden brown all over. You may need to turn them with tongs or a long-handled metal spoon. Drain on crumpled paper towels and season. Serve warm or at room temperature with lemon wedges.

Makes 36

Roast beef on croûtes

10-oz. rib-eye steak
1/3 cup olive oil
2 cloves garlic, crushed
2 sprigs fresh thyme, plus extra
  to garnish
10 slices white bread
1 large clove garlic, peeled, extra

Horseradish cream
1/3 cup heavy whipping cream
1 tablespoon horseradish
1 teaspoon lemon juice

Place the beef in a nonmetallic bowl, add the combined oil, garlic, and thyme, and toss to coat. Cover and chill for 3 hours. Preheat the oven to 400°F.

Cut three rounds from each slice of bread using a 2-inch fluted cutter. Place on a baking sheet and bake for 5 minutes each side, then rub the whole garlic clove over each side of the rounds.

To make the horseradish cream, whisk the cream lightly until thickened. Fold in the horseradish and lemon juice, then season with cracked black pepper. Refrigerate until ready to use.

Heat a roasting pan in the oven for 5 minutes. Season the beef on all sides, then place in the hot roasting pan and turn it so that the surface of the meat is sealed. Drizzle with 2 tablespoons of the reserved marinade, then roast for 10 minutes for rare or until the meat is cooked to your liking. Remove from the oven, cover with aluminum foil, and rest for 15 minutes before slicing thinly.

Arrange a slice of beef on each croûte and top with 1/2 teaspoon of the horseradish cream and a small sprig of thyme. Serve immediately.

Makes 30

Creamed egg with roe tartlets

Basic pastry cases
2 cups all-purpose flour
1/2 cup chilled butter, chopped
1 egg

4 eggs
4 egg yolks
1/3 cup unsalted butter
4 tablespoons roe

Preheat the oven to 400°F. Lightly grease thirty small muffin cups. Sift the flour into a bowl and rub the butter in with your fingertips until the mixture resembles fine breadcrumbs. Make a hollow in the center, add the egg, and mix with a spatula or palette knife, using a cutting action until it comes together in beads. If the dough seems too dry, add a little cold water. Press the dough into a ball on a lightly floured surface, then wrap it in plastic wrap and refrigerate for 30 minutes.

Roll out the dough between two sheets of baking parchment to 1/8 inch thick and cut out thirty rounds with a 2 1/2-inch cutter. Press a round into each muffin cup. Prick the bottoms with a fork and bake for 6–8 minutes or until dry and golden. If they puff up, use a clean dishcloth to press out the air. Allow to cool.

Lightly beat the eggs and egg yolks together. Melt the butter over very low heat, then add the eggs and whisk slowly and constantly for 5–6 minutes or until the mixture is thick and creamy but the eggs are not scrambled. Remove from the heat immediately and season to taste. Fill each pastry case with 1 teaspoon of the creamed egg mixture, then top with 1/2 teaspoon of roe before serving.

Makes 30

Wonton stacks with tuna and ginger

1 1/2 tablespoons sesame seeds
12 fresh wonton wrappers
1/2 cup peanut or vegetable oil
5-oz. tuna fillet (preferably sashimi)
1/4 cup Japanese mayonnaise
  (see Note)
1/4 cup pickled ginger
1 cup snow pea sprouts
2 teaspoons mirin
2 teaspoons soy sauce
1/4 teaspoon sugar

Dry-fry the sesame seeds over low heat for 2–3 minutes or until golden.

Cut the wonton wrappers into quarters to make forty-eight squares. Heat the oil in a small saucepan over medium heat and cook the wrappers in batches for 1–2 minutes or until they are golden and crisp. Drain on crumpled paper towels.

Thinly slice the tuna into twenty-four slices. Spoon approximately 1/4 teaspoon of the mayonnaise onto half of the wonton squares. Place a slice of tuna on the mayonnaise and top with some pickled ginger, snow pea sprouts, and sesame seeds.

Mix the mirin, soy sauce, and sugar together in a small bowl and drizzle a little over each stack. Season with pepper. Top with the remaining wonton squares. Serve immediately, or the stacks will become soggy.

Makes 24

Note: Japanese mayonnaise can be found in Asian markets.
Think ahead: The wonton wrappers can be fried the day before serving. Store them in an airtight container with paper towels between each layer.

Salmon cakes with herb mayonnaise

1-lb. salmon fillet, skin and bones
    removed, cut into ¼-inch cubes
3 tablespoons dry breadcrumbs
1 tablespoon lightly beaten egg
½ teaspoon finely grated lime zest
3½ teaspoons lime juice
3 teaspoons fresh dill, chopped
½ cup mayonnaise
1 clove garlic, crushed
2 tablespoons extra-virgin olive oil

Place the salmon, breadcrumbs, egg, lime zest, 3 teaspoons lime juice, and 2 teaspoons dill in a bowl. Stir until the mixture comes together and the ingredients are evenly distributed. Season well with salt and freshly ground black pepper.

With wet hands, using two heaping teaspoons of mixture at a time, shape into thirty-six small, round cakes. Place on a baking sheet lined with baking parchment. Refrigerate until ready to use.

For the herb mayonnaise, mix the remaining lime juice and dill with the mayonnaise and garlic in a bowl.

Heat the olive oil in a large, nonstick frying pan. Cook the salmon cakes in batches over medium heat for 2 minutes each side or until golden and cooked through. Be careful not to overcook. Drain on paper towels. Top each with some herb mayonnaise and season well. Serve immediately, garnished with lime zest.

Makes 36

Variation: You can also top these with crème fraîche and salmon roe.

Thai chicken sausage rolls

7 oz. boneless, skinless chicken
  breasts, roughly chopped
5 oz. mild pancetta, chopped
1 clove garlic, crushed
3 scallions, chopped
2 tablespoons chopped cilantro
2 bird's-eye chilies, seeded and
  finely chopped
1 teaspoon fish sauce
1 egg
1 teaspoon grated, fresh ginger
12-oz. package frozen puff pastry
1 egg yolk
2 tablespoons sesame seeds
sweet chili sauce, to serve
cilantro, extra, to serve

Preheat the oven to 350°F. Put the chicken, pancetta, garlic, scallions, cilantro, chilies, fish sauce, egg, and ginger in a food processor and process until just combined.

Roll out the pastry to an oblong, 12 x 16 inches. Cut in half lengthwise. Take half the filling, and using floured hands, roll it into a long sausage shape and place along the long edge of one piece of pastry. Brush the edges with a little water and fold over, pressing down to seal. Place the sealed edge underneath. Repeat with the remaining pastry and filling.

Using a sharp knife, cut the sausage rolls into 1 1/4-inch pieces diagonally; discard the end pieces. Brush the tops with egg yolk, then sprinkle with sesame seeds. Bake for 15 minutes or until golden. Serve with sweet chili sauce and garnish with cilantro.

Makes 24

Think ahead: You can make the sausage rolls the day before serving. Reheat in the oven at 350°F for 10 minutes or until warmed through.

Stuffed chilies

1 teaspoon cumin seeds
12 mild, small jalapeño or similar mild,
  oblong, fat chilies, approximately
  1 1/2 x 1 1/4 inches
1 tablespoon olive oil
2 cloves garlic, finely chopped
1/2 small red onion, finely chopped
1/2 cup cream cheese, softened
1/4 cup coarsely grated cheddar
2 tablespoons finely chopped,
  drained, sun-dried tomatoes
1 tablespoon chopped cilantro
1 teaspoon finely chopped lime zest
pinch of paprika
1/2 cup coarse, dry breadcrumbs
2 teaspoons lime juice
cilantro leaves, to garnish

Preheat the oven to 400°F. Line a baking sheet with baking parchment. Dry-fry the cumin seeds for 1–2 minutes or until fragrant. Cool slightly, then grind the seeds.

Cut the chilies lengthwise through the middle. Wearing gloves, remove the seeds and membranes. Bring a saucepan of water to a boil, add the chilies, and cook for 1 minute or until the water comes back to a boil. Drain, rinse under cold water, then return to a saucepan of fresh boiling water for another minute. Drain, rinse, then drain again.

Heat the oil in a nonstick frying pan and cook the garlic and onion over medium-low heat for 4–5 minutes or until the onion softens. Mash the cream cheese in a bowl, add the cheddar, sun-dried tomatoes, cilantro, lime zest, paprika, cumin, and half the breadcrumbs, and mix well. Stir in the onion and season. Fill each chili with one heaping teaspoon of the mixture, then lay on the baking sheet and sprinkle the remaining breadcrumbs over the top.

Bake for 20 minutes. Squeeze some lime juice over the top and garnish with cilantro leaves.

Makes 24

Vegetable dumplings

8 dried shiitake mushrooms
1 tablespoon vegetable oil
2 teaspoons finely chopped, fresh
  ginger
2 garlic cloves, crushed
1 bunch Chinese chives, chopped
3 handfuls water spinach, cut into
  1/2-inch pieces
1/4 cup chicken stock
2 tablespoons oyster sauce
1 tablespoon cornstarch
1 teaspoon soy sauce
1 teaspoon rice wine
1/4 cup water chestnuts, chopped
chili sauce, to serve

Wrappers
1 1/2 cups wheat starch
1 teaspoon cornstarch
vegetable oil, for kneading

Soak the mushrooms in hot water for 15 minutes. Finely chop the caps. Heat the oil in a frying pan over high heat, and add the ginger, garlic, and a pinch of salt and white pepper. Cook for 30 seconds. Add the chives and spinach and cook for 1 minute.

Combine the stock, oyster sauce, cornstarch, soy sauce, and rice wine, and add to the spinach mixture with the water chestnuts and mushrooms. Cook for 1 minute or until thickened, then cool completely.

To make the wrappers, combine the wheat starch and cornstarch. Make a hollow and add 3/4 cup boiling water, a little at a time, bringing the mixture together with your hands. Knead with lightly oiled hands until the dough forms a shiny ball.

Keep the dough covered while you work. Roll out walnut-sized pieces of dough into very thin, 4-inch circles. Place 1 tablespoon of filling in the center. Pinch the edges together to form a tight ball.

Put the dumplings in a bamboo steamer lined with baking parchment, leaving a gap between each one. Cover and steam for 7–8 minutes. Serve with chili sauce.

Makes 24

Hot

Wonton wrapped shrimp

24 medium shrimp
1 teaspoon cornstarch
24 wonton wrappers
vegetable oil, for deep-frying
1/2 cup sweet chili sauce
1 tablespoon lime juice

Peel the shrimp, leaving the tails intact. Pull out the dark vein from each back, starting at the head end.

Mix the cornstarch with 1 teaspoon water in a small bowl. Fold each wonton wrapper in half to form a triangle. Cover them with a dishcloth while you are working, to keep them from drying out. Wrap each shrimp in a wrapper, leaving the tail exposed. Seal at the end by brushing on a little of the cornstarch mixture, then pressing gently. Spread the wrapped shrimp on a baking sheet, cover with plastic wrap, and refrigerate for 20 minutes.

Fill a deep, heavy-bottomed pan one-third full of oil and heat to 350°F or until a cube of bread dropped into the oil browns in 15 seconds. Cook the shrimp in batches for 1 1/2 minutes each batch or until crisp, golden, and cooked through. The cooking time may vary depending on the size of the shrimp. Determine the correct time by cooking one shrimp and testing it before continuing. Remove the shrimp from the oil and drain on crumpled paper towels.

Stir the sweet chili sauce and lime juice together in a small bowl. Serve with the shrimp.

Makes 24

Steamed pork buns

1 cup milk
1/2 cup superfine sugar
3 cups char sui pork bun flour
(see Note)
1 tablespoon vegetable oil

Filling
2 teaspoons vegetable oil
1 clove garlic, crushed
2 scallions, finely chopped
3 teaspoons cornstarch
2 teaspoons hoisin sauce
1 1/2 teaspoons soy sauce
1/2 teaspoon superfine sugar
5 oz. Chinese barbecued pork,
finely chopped

Combine the milk and sugar, and stir over low heat until dissolved. Sift all but two tablespoons of the flour into a bowl and make a hollow. Gradually add the milk, stirring until it just comes together. Dust a work surface with the remaining flour and knead the dough for 10 minutes or until elastic. Knead the oil into the dough a little at a time, kneading for 10 minutes. Cover with plastic wrap and chill for 30 minutes.

For the filling, heat the oil in a pan, add the garlic and scallions, and stir over medium heat until just soft. Blend the cornstarch with 1/3 cup water, the sauces, and sugar, and add to the pan. Stir until the mixture boils and thickens. Remove from the heat and stir in the pork. Allow to cool.

Divide the dough into twenty-four portions and flatten, so the edges are thinner than the center. Put teaspoons of filling on each and pull up the edges around the filling, pinching firmly to seal. Place each bun on a square of baking parchment and place 1 1/4 inches apart in a bamboo steamer. Steam in batches for 15 minutes or until the buns have risen and are cooked through.

Makes about 24

Note: You can find char sui pork bun flour at Asian markets.

Salt and pepper calamari

2 lbs. squid bodies, halved lengthwise
   (see Note)
1 cup lemon juice
1 cup cornstarch
1 1/2 tablespoons salt
1 tablespoon ground white pepper
2 teaspoons superfine sugar
4 egg whites, lightly beaten
vegetable oil, for deep-frying
lemon wedges, for serving

Open out the squid bodies, then wash and pat dry. Lay on a cutting board with the insides facing up. Cut a fine diamond pattern on the inside, being careful not to cut all the way through. Cut the squid into pieces measuring 2 x 3/4 inches. Place in a flat, nonmetallic dish and pour the lemon juice on top. Cover and refrigerate for 15 minutes. Drain well and pat dry.

Combine the cornstarch, salt, white pepper, and sugar in a bowl. Dip the squid into the egg white and lightly coat with the cornstarch mixture, shaking off any excess.

Fill a deep, heavy-bottomed saucepan or deep-fryer one-third full of oil and heat to 350°F or until a cube of bread dropped into the oil turns golden brown in 15 seconds. Deep-fry the squid in batches for 1 minute each batch or until the squid turns lightly golden and curls up. Drain on crumpled paper towels. Serve with lemon wedges.

Serves 12

Note: If you are cleaning the squid yourself, save the tentacles and cut them into groups of two or three depending on the size; marinate and cook them with the bodies.

Mini corn muffins with Cajun fish

Muffins

¾ cup self-rising flour
2 tablespoons cornstarch
½ teaspoon baking powder
½ cup fine cornmeal
2 tablespoons granulated sugar
⅔ cup milk
1 egg
2 tablespoons butter, melted
1 tablespoon butter, extra

Cajun fish

1 teaspoon onion powder
1 teaspoon dried thyme
¾ teaspoon sea salt flakes
½ teaspoon garlic powder
¼ teaspoon cayenne pepper
¼ teaspoon dried oregano
13 oz. firm white fish fillets, skin and
   bones removed
2 tablespoons butter
½ cup sour cream
cilantro leaves, to garnish

Preheat the oven to 350°F. Lightly grease twenty-four small, nonstick muffin cups. Sift the flour, cornstarch, and baking powder into a bowl. Stir in the cornmeal and sugar. Make a hollow in the center. Pour the combined milk and egg into the hollow, then the melted butter. Fold gently with a metal spoon until just combined and still a little lumpy.

Fill each muffin cup about three-quarters full. Bake for 15–20 minutes or until golden. Before removing from the oven, melt the extra butter. Brush the muffins with the butter, then remove from the pan and let cool.

Combine the spices, herbs, and ¼ teaspoon cracked black pepper. Slice the fish into ½-inch slices and coat well in the spice mixture.

Melt the butter in a stainless-steel frying pan (not nonstick) over medium heat and add the fish when the butter is foaming. Cook the fish, turning once, for 1–2 minutes or until it starts to blacken and is cooked.

To serve, cut a small wedge in the top of the muffins, put in ½ teaspoon of sour cream, then add a piece of fish and a cilantro leaf. Serve while the fish is hot.

Makes 24

Arancini

2 cups short-grain rice
1 egg, lightly beaten
1 egg yolk
1/2 cup grated Parmesan
all-purpose flour, to coat
2 eggs, lightly beaten
dry breadcrumbs, to coat
vegetable oil, for deep-frying

Meat sauce
1 dried porcini mushroom
1 tablespoon olive oil
1 onion, chopped
4 oz. ground beef or veal
2 slices prosciutto, finely chopped
2 tablespoons tomato paste
1/3 cup white wine
1/2 teaspoon dried thyme leaves
3 tablespoons finely chopped,
  fresh parsley

Cook the rice in boiling water for
20 minutes or until just soft. Drain,
without rinsing, and cool. Put in
a large bowl and add the egg, egg
yolk, and Parmesan. Stir until the rice
sticks together. Cover and set aside.

To make the meat sauce, soak the
mushroom in hot water for 10 minutes
to soften, then squeeze dry and chop
finely. Heat the oil in a frying pan. Add
the mushroom and onion, and cook
for 3 minutes or until soft. Add the
ground meat and cook, stirring, until
browned. Add the prosciutto, tomato
paste, wine, thyme, and pepper to
taste. Cook, stirring, for 5 minutes or
until all the liquid is absorbed. Stir in
the parsley and set aside to cool.

With wet hands, form the rice mixture
into ten balls. Wet your hands again
and gently pull the balls apart. Place
3 teaspoons of the meat sauce in the
center of each. Reshape to enclose
the filling. Roll in the flour, beaten egg,
and breadcrumbs, and chill for 1 hour.

Fill a deep, heavy-bottomed pan
one-third full of oil and heat to 350°F
or until a cube of bread browns in
15 seconds. Deep-fry the croquettes,
two at a time, for 3–4 minutes or until
golden brown. Drain on paper towels
and keep warm while cooking the rest.

Makes 10

Lentil patties with cumin skordalia

1 cup brown lentils
1 teaspoon cumin seeds
$1/2$ cup bulgur wheat
1 tablespoon olive oil
3 cloves garlic, crushed
4 scallions, thinly sliced
1 teaspoon ground coriander
3 tablespoons chopped, fresh parsley
3 tablespoons chopped, fresh mint
2 eggs, lightly beaten
vegetable oil, for deep-frying

Skordalia
1 lb. russet potatoes, cut into $3/4$-inch
  cubes
3 cloves garlic, crushed
$1/2$ teaspoon ground cumin
pinch of ground white pepper
$3/4$ cup olive oil
2 tablespoons white vinegar

Place the lentils in a saucepan, add $2^1/2$ cups water, and bring to a boil. Reduce the heat to low and cook, covered, for 30 minutes or until soft. Meanwhile, dry-fry the cumin over low heat for 1–2 minutes or until fragrant. Grind.

Remove the lentils from the heat and stir in the bulgur wheat. Allow to cool.

Heat the oil in a frying pan and cook the garlic and scallions for 1 minute. Add the coriander and cumin, and cook for 30 seconds. Add to the lentil mixture with the parsley, mint, and egg. Mix well. Chill for 30 minutes.

To make the skordalia, boil the potatoes for 10 minutes or until very soft. Drain and mash until smooth. Add the garlic, cumin, white pepper, and 1 teaspoon salt. Gradually add the oil, mixing with a wooden spoon. Add the vinegar.

Roll tablespoons of the lentil mixture into balls, then flatten slightly. Fill a deep, heavy-bottomed saucepan or deep-fryer one-third full of oil and heat to 350°F or until a cube of bread browns in 15 seconds. Cook the patties in batches for 1–2 minutes or until crisp and browned. Drain on paper towels. Serve with the skordalia.

Makes 32

Scallops on potato chips with pea puree

1 tablespoon butter
3 shallots, finely chopped
1 clove garlic, finely chopped
2 slices mild pancetta, finely chopped
1 cup frozen peas
1/4 cup chicken stock or water
vegetable oil, for deep-frying,
   plus 1 tablespoon extra
4–5 russet potatoes, peeled and
   sliced very thinly to make 48 slices
24 scallops, cut in half horizontally
   through the center
fresh mint

Melt the butter in a small saucepan and fry the shallots, garlic, and pancetta over low heat for 3 minutes or until soft but not browned. Add the peas and stock, and cook over high heat for 3 minutes or until all the liquid has evaporated. Cool a little, transfer to a food processor, and puree until smooth. Season.

Fill a deep, heavy-bottomed saucepan or deep-fryer one-third full of oil and heat to 375°F or until a cube of bread dropped into the oil browns in 10 seconds. Cook the potato slices in batches until crisp and golden. Drain on crumpled paper towels and sprinkle with salt.

Toss the scallops with 1 tablespoon oil. Season lightly. Heat a ridged grill pan until hot, then sear the scallops in batches for 5 seconds each side or until lightly browned on the outside but opaque in the middle.

Reheat the pea puree. Put a teaspoon of puree on each potato chip, then top with a scallop. Season with pepper and garnish with mint.

Makes 48

Think ahead: The puree can be made 2 days before and refrigerated. The chips can be cooked 2 hours before and stored in an airtight container.

Bitterballen

1¾ cups beef stock
1 small carrot, very finely diced
½ celery stalk, very finely diced
1 small onion, very finely diced
1 bay leaf
¼ cup butter
½ cup all-purpose flour
10 oz. ground beef or veal
3 cloves garlic, crushed
1 tablespoon finely chopped,
  fresh parsley
1 tablespoon Worcestershire sauce
2 teaspoons ground nutmeg
1 teaspoon lemon zest, finely minced
dry breadcrumbs, to coat
3 eggs, beaten
vegetable oil, for deep-frying
English mustard, to serve

Place the stock, carrot, celery, onion, and bay leaf in a saucepan and bring to a boil over high heat. Simmer for 10 minutes. Strain, saving all the solids except the bay leaf.

Melt the butter over medium heat in a large saucepan. Add the flour, mix well, and cook for 1 minute. Gradually add the warm stock, stirring constantly until you have a thick, smooth sauce. Reduce the heat to low.

Add the ground beef, garlic, parsley, Worcestershire sauce, nutmeg, lemon zest, reserved vegetables, 1 teaspoon salt, and ½ teaspoon cracked black pepper. Cook over low heat for 15 minutes, stirring regularly. Cool slightly, then transfer to a clean dish. Cover and chill overnight or until the mixture is well chilled and firm.

Shape heaping teaspoons of the mixture into balls. Roll in breadcrumbs, then in egg, then again in breadcrumbs. Chill the finished balls as you work. Refrigerate for 1 hour.

Fill a large, heavy-bottomed saucepan one-third full of oil and heat to 375°F or until a cube of bread browns in 10 seconds. Deep-fry the balls for 4 minutes or until golden. Serve immediately with mustard.

Makes about 60

Honey mustard chicken drumettes

⅓ cup vegetable oil
¼ cup honey
¼ cup soy sauce
¼ cup Dijon mustard
¼ cup lemon juice
4 cloves garlic, crushed
24 chicken drumettes (see Note)

To make the marinade, place the oil, honey, soy sauce, mustard, lemon juice, and garlic in a large, nonmetallic dish and mix together thoroughly.

Trim the chicken of excess fat, then place in the dish with the marinade and toss until well coated. Cover and refrigerate for at least 2 hours or preferably overnight, turning 2–3 times.

Preheat the oven to 400°F. Lay the drumettes on a wire rack that has been placed over a baking sheet lined with aluminum foil. Bake, turning and brushing with the marinade 3–4 times, for 45 minutes or until golden brown and cooked. Serve immediately.

Makes 24

Note: Drumettes are the chicken wing with the wing tip removed.
Think ahead: Cook a day ahead and reheat in an oven at 315°F for 10–12 minutes.
Variation: For a teriyaki marinade, combine ½ cup teriyaki sauce, ¼ cup pineapple juice, 2 tablespoons honey, 1 tablespoon grated, fresh ginger, 2 cloves crushed garlic, and 1 teaspoon sesame oil.

Spinach and feta triangles

2 lbs. spinach
1/4 cup olive oil
1 onion, chopped
10 scallions, sliced
1/3 cup chopped, fresh parsley
1 tablespoon chopped, fresh dill
large pinch of ground nutmeg
1/3 cup grated Parmesan
1 cup crumbled feta
1/3 cup ricotta
4 eggs, lightly beaten
3 tablespoons butter, melted
1 tablespoon olive oil, extra
12 sheets phyllo pastry

Trim any stems from the spinach. Wash the leaves, leaving them wet, roughly chop, and place in a saucepan. Cover and cook over low heat for 5 minutes or until wilted. Drain and allow to cool before squeezing to remove excess water.

Heat the oil in a heavy-bottomed frying pan. Add the onion and cook over low heat for 10 minutes or until tender and golden. Add the scallions and cook for another 3 minutes. Remove from the heat. Stir in the spinach, parsley, dill, nutmeg, Parmesan, feta, ricotta, and eggs. Season well.

Preheat the oven to 350°F. Grease two baking sheets. Combine the butter with the extra oil. Work with three sheets of pastry at a time, covering the rest with a damp dishcloth. Brush each sheet with butter mixture and lay them on top of each other. Halve lengthwise.

Place 4 tablespoons of filling on an angle at the end of each strip. Fold the pastry to enclose the filling and form a triangle. Continue folding the triangle over until you reach the end. Brush with the remaining butter mixture and bake for 20 minutes or until golden brown.

Makes 8

Macadamia-crusted chicken strips

12 chicken tenderloins (1½ lbs.),
  larger ones cut in half
seasoned all-purpose flour, to dust
2 eggs, lightly beaten
1¾ cups macadamias, finely
  chopped
2 cups fresh breadcrumbs
vegetable oil, for deep-frying

Cut the chicken into strips. Dust the chicken strips with the flour, then dip them in the egg and coat them in the combined nuts and breadcrumbs. Refrigerate for at least 30 minutes.

Fill a large, heavy-bottomed saucepan or deep-fryer one-third full of oil and heat to 350°F or until a cube of bread browns in 15 seconds. Cook the chicken in batches for 2–3 minutes or until golden brown all over, being careful not to burn the nuts. Drain on crumpled paper towels. Serve warm.

Makes 24

Variations: The chicken strips are very tasty served with sweet chili sauce or a mango salsa. Try making your own salsa by combining a small, finely diced mango, 2 tablespoons finely diced red onion, 2 tablespoons roughly chopped cilantro leaves, a fresh green chili that has been seeded and finely chopped, and 1 tablespoon of lime juice. Season to taste. Try a different coating using almonds or peanuts.

Spicy corn puffs

2 ears of corn
3 tablespoons chopped cilantro
  leaves
6 scallions, finely chopped
1 small, fresh red chili, seeded and
  finely chopped
1 large egg
2 teaspoons ground cumin
$\frac{1}{2}$ teaspoon ground coriander
1 cup all-purpose flour
vegetable oil, for deep-frying
sweet chili sauce, to serve

Cut down the side of the corn with a sharp knife to release the kernels. Roughly chop the kernels, then place them in a large bowl. Holding the ears over the bowl, scrape down the sides with a knife to release any corn juice into the bowl.

Add the cilantro, scallions, chili, egg, cumin, ground coriander, 1 teaspoon salt, and some cracked black pepper to the bowl and stir well. Add the flour and mix well. The texture of the batter will vary depending on the juiciness of the corn. If the mixture is too dry, add 1 tablespoon water, but no more than that, as the batter should be quite dry. Allow to rest for 10 minutes.

Fill a large, heavy-bottomed saucepan or deep-fryer one-third full of oil and heat to 350°F or until a cube of bread dropped in the oil browns in 15 seconds. Drop slightly heaping teaspoons of the corn batter into the oil and cook for 1$\frac{1}{2}$ minutes or until puffed and golden. Drain on crumpled paper towels and serve immediately with a bowl of the sweet chili sauce for dipping.

Makes about 36

Note: The corn puffs should be prepared just before serving.

Sesame beef skewers

1/2 cup soy sauce
1/3 cup Chinese rice wine
2 cloves garlic, crushed
1 teaspoon finely grated, fresh ginger
1 teaspoon sesame oil
7-oz. rib-eye steak, cut into
   3/4-inch cubes
8 scallions
2 tablespoons toasted sesame seeds

Combine the soy sauce, wine, garlic, ginger, and oil, and pour over the beef. Marinate for 20 minutes. Drain, saving the marinade.

Cut six of the scallions into 1 1/4-inch pieces and thread a piece plus two meat cubes onto a skewer. Cook on a hot, ridged grill pan for 5 minutes or until cooked. Remove from the pan, sprinkle with sesame seeds, and keep warm.

Put the marinade in a saucepan and bring to a boil for 1 minute, then add 2 thinly sliced scallions. Pour into a bowl and serve with the skewers.

Makes 24

Basil mussels

2 lbs. black mussels
1/2 tablespoon butter
2 red Asian shallots, chopped
1/2 cup dry white wine

Basil butter
1/4 cup butter
1/3 cup fresh basil leaves
1 clove garlic, chopped
2 tablespoons dry breadcrumbs

Scrub the mussels with a stiff brush and pull out the hairy beards. Discard any broken mussels or open ones that don't close when tapped on the counter. Rinse well.

Melt the butter in a large saucepan over medium heat. Add the shallots and cook for 2 minutes or until soft. Add the wine and mussels, increase the heat, and cook for 4–5 minutes, stirring occasionally, until the mussels have opened. Remove the open mussels and discard unopened ones.

For the basil butter, process all the ingredients together in a food processor or blender until smooth. Season with ground black pepper.

Separate the mussel shells, leaving the meat on one half. Discard the empty shells. Place a teaspoon of basil butter on each mussel. Arrange on a broiler pan lined with aluminum foil and cook under a hot broiler for 1 minute or until the butter is melted. Season to taste with salt and pepper.

Serves 6

Variation: Use scallops on the shell— remove the hard muscle and continue from step 3. Broil for 2 minutes.

Hot

Turkish bread with herbed zucchini

½ large loaf Turkish bread
1 tablespoon sesame seeds
½ cup vegetable oil

Herbed zucchini
1 tablespoon olive oil
2 cloves garlic, finely chopped
4 small zucchini, roughly chopped
1 large carrot, thinly sliced
2 tablespoons chopped, fresh
  Italian parsley
2 tablespoons chopped, fresh mint
2 teaspoons lemon juice
½ teaspoon ground cumin

Split the bread horizontally through the middle and open it out. Cut the bread into 1¼-inch squares—you should have forty-eight squares.

Dry-fry the sesame seeds in a large, nonstick frying pan over low heat for 2–3 minutes or until golden. Remove from the pan. Heat the vegetable oil in the same pan and cook the bread in batches for 1–2 minutes each side or until crisp and golden. Drain on paper towels.

Heat the olive oil in a saucepan over medium heat and cook the garlic for 1 minute. Add the zucchini and carrot, and cook over medium heat for 2 minutes. Season with salt and pepper. Add 1 tablespoon water, cover, and simmer over low heat for 15 minutes or until the vegetables are soft. Spoon into a bowl and mash roughly with a potato masher. Add the parsley, mint, lemon juice, and cumin. Season to taste.

Spoon 2 teaspoons of the zucchini mixture over each square of bread and sprinkle with sesame seeds. Serve warm or at room temperature.

Makes 48

Think ahead: The herbed zucchini can be prepared up to 2 days in advance. Reheat just before serving.

Caramelized red onion and feta tartlets

1 1/2 tablespoons olive oil
2 large red onions, finely chopped
2 teaspoons chopped, fresh thyme
3 sheets store-bought, short-crust pastry
1/2 cup feta, crumbled
2 eggs, lightly beaten
1/2 cup whipping cream

Preheat the oven to 350°F. Heat the oil in a frying pan (don't use a nonstick one or the onions won't caramelize). Add the onions and cook, stirring occasionally, over medium-low heat for 30 minutes or until dark gold. Add the thyme, stir well, and transfer to a bowl to cool.

Grease twenty-four shallow, tart pan cups. Using an 3-inch cutter, cut out twenty-four pastry rounds and line the cups with the rounds.

Divide the onions among the tart cups, then spoon the feta over the onions. Combine the eggs with the cream, season, and pour into the pastry cases. Bake for 10–15 minutes or until puffed and golden. Leave in the pan for 5 minutes before transferring to a wire rack to cool.

Makes 24

Think ahead: These can be made the day before and reheated in a 300°F oven for 10 minutes before serving.

Herring fritters with tartar sauce

1 cup all-purpose flour
1 large egg, lightly beaten
1 cup ice water
3 tablespoons chopped, fresh parsley
3 teaspoons grated lemon zest
13 oz. herring
vegetable oil, for deep-frying

Tartar sauce
2 egg yolks
1 teaspoon Dijon mustard
1 cup olive oil
1 tablespoon lemon juice
2 tablespoons capers, drained and
  chopped
2 tablespoons chopped gherkins
1 tablespoon chopped, fresh parsley
1 tablespoon chopped, fresh tarragon

Sift the flour and a pinch of salt and pepper into a large bowl, make a hollow in the center, and add the egg. Whisk gently and gradually add the water, stirring constantly until the batter is smooth. Stir in the parsley and lemon zest. Cover and refrigerate for 1 hour.

To make the tartar sauce, place the egg yolks and mustard in a food processor and pulse for 10 seconds. While processing, slowly add the oil in a thin stream until the mixture is thick and creamy. Add the lemon juice and 2 teaspoons boiling water and pulse for another 10 seconds. Transfer to a bowl, add the capers, gherkins, parsley, and tarragon, and season generously. Cover and refrigerate until needed.

Pat the herring dry, then gently stir into the batter. Fill a large, heavy-bottomed saucepan one-third full of oil and heat to 375°F or until a cube of bread dropped in the oil browns in 10 seconds. Put small tablespoons of batter into the oil. Cook the fritters in batches, gently tossing in the oil. Cook for 2 minutes or until the fritters are golden brown. Drain on crumpled paper towels and keep warm. Repeat with the remaining mixture. Serve immediately with the tartar sauce.

Makes 50

Steamed shrimp rice noodle rolls

Dipping sauce
2 tablespoons light soy sauce
3 tablespoons rice vinegar

3 dried shiitake mushrooms
$3/4$ lb. shrimp, peeled and deveined
4 scallions, chopped
$2/3$ cup chopped snow peas
2 teaspoons finely chopped,
 fresh ginger
2 cloves garlic, crushed
$1/2$ cup chopped cilantro leaves
$1/2$ cup water chestnuts, chopped
1 teaspoon sesame oil
1 tablespoon light soy sauce
1 egg white
1 teaspoon cornstarch
10 oz. fresh rice sheet noodles

To make the dipping sauce, combine the soy sauce and rice vinegar.

Cover the mushrooms with hot water and soak for 15 minutes. Drain, discard the stems, and finely chop the caps.

Mince the shrimp in a food processor. Add the mushrooms, scallions, snow peas, ginger, garlic, cilantro, water chestnuts, sesame oil, soy sauce, and a pinch of salt. Add the egg white and cornstarch, and pulse until smooth.

Line a large bamboo steamer with baking parchment and place over a wok of simmering water (make sure the bottom doesn't touch the water). Gently unfold the rice sheet noodle and cut into six 6-inch squares. Spread $1/4$ cup of filling evenly over each square and roll firmly to form a log. Steam, covered, in a wok for 5 minutes. Cut each roll in half and serve with the sauce.

Makes 12

Rosti with smoked trout and salsa verde

1 small smoked trout
1 lb. russet potatoes
2 scallions, thinly sliced
1/3 cup olive oil

Salsa verde
1 1/2 cups fresh Italian parsley
1 cup fresh basil
1 tablespoon capers, drained
1 tablespoon chopped gherkin or
   4 cornichons (baby gherkins)
2 anchovies, drained
1 clove garlic, chopped
2 teaspoons Dijon mustard
1/4 cup olive oil
1 tablespoon lemon juice

Remove the skin from the trout, pull the flesh from the bones, and flake into pieces.

To make the salsa verde, place the parsley, basil, capers, gherkin, anchovies, garlic, and mustard in a food processor and blend until finely chopped. While processing, blend in the oil and lemon juice until mixed together. Season with pepper.

To make the rosti, peel and coarsely grate the potatoes. Squeeze out as much liquid as possible. Mix the flesh in a bowl with the scallions. Heat the oil in a large, heavy-bottomed frying pan over medium-high heat. To cook the rosti, take heaping teaspoons of the potato mixture, add to the pan in batches, and press down with a spatula to help the potatoes stay together. Cook for 2–3 minutes each side or until crisp and golden. Drain on crumpled paper towels.

Top each rosti with a teaspoon of salsa verde and some trout. Serve warm or at room temperature.

Makes 32

Think ahead: The rosti can be made 8 hours beforehand and kept in an airtight container lined with paper towels. Reheat for 5 minutes in a 350°F oven.

Polenta wedges with bocconcini and tomatoes

1 tablespoon olive oil
1$^2/_3$ cups polenta
$^3/_4$ cup grated Parmesan
2$^1/_2$ tablespoons pesto
1 cup thinly sliced bocconcini
   (fresh mozzarella)
12 cherry tomatoes, cut into quarters
$^1/_2$ cup fresh basil, larger leaves torn

Lightly grease an 8 x 12-inch baking pan with the olive oil. Bring 4 cups lightly salted water to a boil in a saucepan. Once the water is boiling, add the polenta in a steady stream, stirring continuously to keep lumps from forming. Reduce the heat to very low and simmer, stirring, for 20–25 minutes or until the polenta starts to come away from the sides of the pan.

Stir the Parmesan into the polenta and season with salt and pepper. Spoon the polenta into the baking pan, smooth the top with the back of a wet spoon, and leave for 1 hour or until set.

Once the polenta has set, carefully transfer it onto a cutting board and cut into twenty-four 2-inch squares. Cut each square into two triangles. Cook the polenta in batches on a preheated, ridged grill pan for 2–3 minutes on each side or until warmed through.

Spread each triangle with 1 teaspoon of the pesto, then top with a slice of bocconcini and a tomato quarter. Season and toast under the broiler for 1–2 minutes or until the cheese is just starting to melt. Garnish with basil and serve immediately.

Makes 48

Shrimp and pesto pizza

Pizza dough
1/4-oz. packet active dry yeast
1/2 teaspoon superfine sugar
2 cups all-purpose flour
1 tablespoon olive oil

2 tablespoons olive oil
1 teaspoon finely chopped, fresh basil
1 clove garlic, crushed
24 cooked, medium shrimp, peeled
  and deveined
1/4 cup pesto
24 small, fresh basil leaves
24 pine nuts

Combine the yeast, sugar, and 3/4 cup warm water, cover, and leave for 10 minutes or until frothy. If it hasn't foamed after 10 minutes, discard and start again.

Sift the flour and 1/2 teaspoon salt together and make a hollow. Add the yeast mixture and the oil. Mix with a rubber spatula or palette knife, using a cutting action, until a dough forms. Turn onto a floured surface and knead for 10 minutes or until smooth. Transfer to an oiled bowl, cover with plastic wrap, and leave for 45 minutes or until doubled in size. Meanwhile, mix the oil, basil, garlic, and shrimp in a nonmetallic bowl. Cover with plastic wrap and refrigerate for 30 minutes.

Preheat the oven to 450°F. Punch down the dough, then knead for 8 minutes or until elastic. Divide into twenty-four balls and roll each ball into a circle 1/4 inch thick and 1 3/4 inches in diameter. Prick the surfaces with a fork and brush with oil.

Place the bases on a lightly greased baking sheet. Spread 1/2 teaspoon of pesto over each base, leaving a narrow border. Put a shrimp, basil leaf, and pine nut on each pizza and bake for 8–10 minutes.

Makes 24

Satay chicken sticks

8 large chicken tenderloins, trimmed
   and sliced into thirds lengthwise
1 clove garlic, crushed
3 teaspoons fish sauce
2 teaspoons grated fresh ginger
24 kaffir lime leaves
lime quarters, to serve

Satay sauce
2 teaspoons peanut oil
4 red Asian shallots, finely chopped
2 cloves garlic, chopped
2 teaspoons grated, fresh ginger
2 small, fresh red chilies, finely
   chopped
$3/4$ cup coconut milk
$1/2$ cup crunchy peanut butter
2 tablespoons light brown sugar
2 tablespoons lime juice
$11/2$ tablespoons fish sauce
2 teaspoons soy sauce
1 fresh kaffir lime leaf

Combine the chicken, garlic, fish
sauce, and ginger. Cover, then
refrigerate for 1 hour.

To make the sauce, heat the oil
in a saucepan over medium heat.
Add the shallots, garlic, ginger, and
chilies, and cook for 5 minutes or
until golden. Add the rest of the
ingredients, reduce the heat, and
simmer for 10 minutes or until thick.

Thread a lime leaf and chicken strip
onto each skewer. Cook on a hot,
ridged grill pan for 3–4 minutes. Serve
with satay sauce and lime wedges.

Makes 24

Sweet potato and lentil pastry moneybags

2 tablespoons olive oil
1 large leek, finely chopped
2 cloves garlic, crushed
1 1/2 cups button mushrooms, roughly
  chopped
2 teaspoons ground cumin
2 teaspoons ground coriander
1/2 cup brown or green lentils
1/2 cup red lentils
2 cups vegetable stock
3/4 lb. sweet potatoes, diced
4 tablespoons finely chopped
  cilantro leaves
8 sheets store-bought puff pastry
1 egg, lightly beaten
1/2 leek, extra, cut into 1/4-inch-wide
  strips
3/4 cup plain yogurt
2 tablespoons grated cucumber
1/2 teaspoon light brown sugar

Preheat the oven to 400°F. Heat the oil in a saucepan over medium heat and cook the leek for 2–3 minutes or until soft. Add the garlic, mushrooms, cumin, and ground coriander, and cook for 1 minute or until fragrant.

Add the combined lentils and stock and bring to a boil. Reduce the heat and simmer for 20–25 minutes or until the lentils are cooked through, stirring occasionally. Add the sweet potatoes in the last 5 minutes.

Transfer to a bowl and stir in the cilantro. Season to taste. Cool.

Cut the pastry sheets into four even squares. Place 1 1/2 tablespoons of filling into the center of each square and bring the edges together to form a moneybag. Pinch together, then tie each moneybag with string. Lightly brush with egg and place on lined baking sheets. Bake for 20 minutes or until the pastry is puffed and golden.

Soak the leek strips in boiling water for 30 seconds. Remove the string and retie with a piece of blanched leek. Put the yogurt, cucumber, and sugar in a bowl and mix together well. Serve with the moneybags.

Makes 32

Thai fish cakes with dipping sauce

1 lb. firm, white fish fillets, skin
  removed
1 1/2 tablespoons red curry paste
1/4 cup granulated sugar
1/4 cup fish sauce
1 egg
1 cup thinly sliced snake beans
10 fresh kaffir lime leaves, finely
  chopped
vegetable oil, for deep-frying

Dipping sauce
1/2 cup sugar
1/4 cup white vinegar
1 tablespoon fish sauce
1 small, fresh red chili, chopped
2 tablespoons finely chopped carrot
2 tablespoons peeled, seeded, and
  finely chopped cucumber
1 tablespoon roasted peanuts,
  chopped

Place the fish in a food processor and process until smooth. Add the curry paste, sugar, fish sauce, and egg. Process for another 10 seconds or until combined. Stir in the beans and chopped lime leaves.

Shape the mixture into walnut-size balls, then flatten them into patties.

Fill a wok one-third full of oil and heat to 350°F or until a cube of bread dropped into the oil browns in 15 seconds. Cook in batches for 3–5 minutes, turning occasionally. Drain on crumpled paper towels.

To make the dipping sauce, place the sugar, vinegar, fish sauce, chili, and 1/2 cup water in a saucepan. Simmer for 5 minutes or until thickened slightly. Cool. Stir in the chopped carrot, cucumber, and peanuts. Serve the dipping sauce with the fish cakes.

Makes 24

Think ahead: The fish cakes can be prepared, shaped, and placed on baking sheets lined with plastic wrap and kept in the refrigerator a day ahead. Cook them just before serving.

Burgundy beef pies

Filling
2 tablespoons olive oil
1 lb. diced lean beef (round)
1 onion, finely chopped
2 oz. pancetta, finely chopped
2 cloves garlic, crushed
1 tablespoon tomato paste
1 cup red wine
$\frac{1}{2}$ cup beef stock
1 teaspoon dried Italian herbs
$\frac{1}{2}$ cup pureed tomatoes

$1\frac{1}{2}$ lbs. store-bought short-crust pastry
1 egg, lightly beaten

Heat half the oil in a large saucepan and cook the beef in batches over high heat for 5 minutes or until browned. Remove the meat and set aside. Add the remaining oil and cook the onion, pancetta, and garlic for 3–4 minutes or until soft. Return the meat to the saucepan, stir in the rest of the ingredients, cover, and simmer for 50–60 minutes or until the meat is tender. Remove the lid and cook for another 30 minutes or until the sauce is reduced. Allow to cool.

Preheat the oven to 350°F and put a baking sheet in the oven. Grease twenty-four mini muffin cups. Roll the pastry thinly and cut out twenty-four rounds with a $2\frac{3}{4}$-inch cutter. Repeat with a $2\frac{1}{4}$-inch cutter. Put one of the larger rounds in each muffin cup and fill with the cooled filling. Dampen the edges of the small rounds and place them on top of the filling to seal the pies. Brush with egg. Put the muffin pan on the hot baking sheet and cook for 25 minutes or until golden. Cool slightly, then remove from the pan.

Makes 24

Vegetable pakoras with minty yogurt sauce

1 cup plain yogurt
1 cup fresh mint
2 tablespoons coriander seeds
1 tablespoon cumin seeds
1½ cups besan (chickpea flour)
  (see Note)
1½ teaspoons chili powder
1 teaspoon ground turmeric
3 tablespoons finely chopped cilantro
1 teaspoon vegetable oil
3¼ cups cauliflower florets, cut into
  ½-inch pieces
1 small onion, thinly sliced
1 cup grated zucchini
1 clove garlic, crushed
vegetable oil, for deep-frying
lemon wedges, to serve

To make the dipping sauce, put the yogurt and mint in a food processor and pulse for 10–20 seconds or until the mint is thoroughly chopped.

Dry-fry the coriander and cumin seeds in a frying pan over low heat for 2–3 minutes or until fragrant. Cool slightly, then grind to a powder. Transfer to a large bowl and add the besan, chili powder, turmeric, cilantro, and 1 teaspoon salt. Mix well, stir in the oil, then gradually add ⅔ cup warm water and stir until a smooth, thick paste forms. Mix the cauliflower, onion, grated zucchini, and garlic into the batter.

Fill a deep, heavy-bottomed saucepan one-third full of oil and heat to 350°F or until a cube of bread browns in 15 seconds. Carefully add 1 tablespoon of the batter to the oil, then repeat until you are cooking five pakoras at a time. Cook each batch for 2 minutes each side or until golden. Drain on paper towels. Sprinkle with salt and repeat with the remaining mixture. Serve hot with yogurt sauce and lemon wedges.

Makes 40

Note: Besan is available from Asian markets.

Mini spicy pork quesadillas

2¾ tablespoons olive oil
½ teaspoon ground oregano
1 teaspoon ground cumin
½ teaspoon garlic salt
½ teaspoon cayenne pepper
11 oz. ground pork
2–3 chopped jalapeño chilies in brine
¼ cup pitted black olives, sliced
⅓ cup green olives stuffed with red
  pimientos, sliced
2 tablespoons chopped cilantro
  leaves
5 6½-inch flour tortillas
½ cup grated, mild cheddar
½ cup grated mozzarella
fresh cilantro sprigs, to garnish

To make the spicy ground pork, heat 1½ tablespoons of the olive oil in a large frying pan. When hot, add the oregano, cumin, garlic salt, and cayenne pepper, and cook for 30 seconds. Add the ground pork and cook over high heat for 10 minutes before incorporating the chilies and all the olives. Cook for another 5 minutes, then stir in the chopped cilantro. Remove from the heat and allow to cool.

Cut each tortilla in half. Place 1 tablespoon of filling on one side of each half. Mix the cheeses together, then put 1 tablespoon of the grated cheese on top of the spicy ground pork. Turn the flap of tortilla over the filling and press down firmly.

Heat 2 teaspoons of the remaining oil in a nonstick frying pan over high heat and cook the quesadillas in batches of six for 3–4 minutes each side or until golden. Add a teaspoon of oil to the pan after each batch. Garnish with cilantro sprigs.

Makes 24

Variation: For a very simple vegetarian filling, simply sprinkle each half of the tortilla with 1 tablespoon chopped tomato, chili, olives, and cilantro, then the cheese; fold over and cook as for the pork quesadillas.

Shrimp potstickers

Dipping sauce
¼ cup soy sauce
1 scallion, thinly sliced
1 clove garlic, crushed
¼ teaspoon finely chopped,
  fresh ginger
¼ teaspoon sesame oil

1 lb. medium shrimp
1 cup Napa cabbage, finely shredded
¼ cup drained, finely chopped
  water chestnuts
1 tablespoon finely chopped
  cilantro leaves
24 round gow gee wrappers
  (see Note)
1 tablespoon vegetable oil
½ cup chicken stock

To make the dipping sauce, mix together all the ingredients in a small bowl.

Peel and devein the shrimp, then chop finely. Combine the shrimp meat, cabbage, water chestnuts, and cilantro.

Lay all the gow gee wrappers out on a work surface and put one heaping teaspoon of the shrimp filling in the center of each. Moisten the edges with water and draw together into the shape of a purse, pressing the edges together firmly to seal.

Heat the oil in a large frying pan and add the potstickers. Cook in batches over medium heat for 2 minutes or until just brown on the bottom. Add the stock, then quickly cover with a lid to prevent spattering. Steam for 2–3 minutes, making sure that all the stock does not evaporate and the potstickers do not burn. Serve immediately with the dipping sauce.

Makes 24

Note: Gow gee wrappers are rolled-out, round pieces of dough made from wheat flour and water. They are available from Asian markets.

Mediterranean twists

2 tablespoons olive oil
2 onions, thinly sliced
1/3 cup dry white wine
3 teaspoons sugar
1 cup chopped, fresh Italian parsley
8 anchovies, drained and finely
  chopped
1 cup coarsely grated Gruyère cheese
6 sheets phyllo pastry
1/4 cup unsalted butter, melted

Preheat the oven to 425°F and warm a baking sheet. Heat the oil in a frying pan and cook the onions over low heat for 5 minutes. Add the wine and sugar and cook for 10–15 minutes or until the onions are golden. Remove from the heat and cool.

Combine the parsley with the cheese, anchovies, and cooled onions.

Keeping the phyllo pastry covered while you work, take one sheet, brush lightly with the butter, cover with another sheet, and repeat until you have three buttered sheets. Spread the parsley mixture over the pastry and top with the remaining three sheets, buttering each layer as before. Press down firmly, then cut the pastry in half widthwise, then cut each half into strips 1/2–3/4 inch wide. Brush with butter, then gently twist each strip. Lightly season with black pepper, place on a baking sheet, and bake for 10–15 minutes or until golden.

Makes 24

Think ahead: Make the twists up to 2 days beforehand and store them in an airtight container. Warm them in a 350°F oven for 10 minutes before serving.

Mini steak sandwiches

1/3 cup olive oil
1 onion, thinly sliced
3/4 cup fresh parsley
10 large, fresh basil leaves
20 fresh mint leaves
1 clove garlic, crushed
1 tablespoon Dijon mustard
1 tablespoon capers
2 anchovy fillets
13-oz. steak fillet, about 1/2 inch thick
1 baguette, cut into 40 1/4-inch slices

Heat 2 tablespoons of oil in a frying pan and cook the onion over low heat for 25 minutes or until caramelized.

To make the salsa verde, place the parsley, basil, mint, garlic, mustard, capers, anchovies, and the remaining oil in a food processor, and pulse to a thick paste. Season.

Cut out twenty rounds from the steak with a 1-inch cutter. Season, then sear on a lightly oiled, ridged grill pan on both sides for 1–2 minutes or until cooked to your liking. Put a little of the onion on twenty rounds of bread, top with a piece of steak and a dollop of salsa verde, then top with the remaining bread. Serve warm.

Makes 20

Gyoza

10 oz. ground pork
5½ cups finely shredded and lightly
  blanched Napa cabbage with the
  excess water squeezed out
1 bunch fresh Chinese chives,
  chopped
1 tablespoon finely chopped, fresh
  ginger
¼ cup soy sauce
1 tablespoon rice wine
1 teaspoon sugar
45 wonton wrappers
2 teaspoons vegetable oil

Dipping sauce
2 tablespoons soy sauce
1 tablespoon black Chinese vinegar
1 teaspoon sesame oil
½ teaspoon chili oil

Combine the ground pork, Napa
cabbage, Chinese chives, and ginger
in a bowl. Add the soy sauce, rice
wine, sugar, and 1 teaspoon salt
and mix together very well.

Place a gow gee wrapper flat in
the palm of your hand, then place
2 teaspoons of the filling mixture into
the center of the wrapper. With wet
fingers, bring the sides together to
form a half-moon shape and pinch
the seam firmly to seal it in a pleat.

Press one side of the dumplings onto
a flat surface to create a flat bottom;
this will make the dumplings easier
to fry.

Heat the oil in a frying pan over
medium-high heat. Add the gyoza
to the pan in batches and cook for
1–2 minutes on the flat side, without
moving, so that the gyoza become
brown and crisp on that side. Transfer
to a plate. Return the gyoza to the
pan in batches, then gradually add
⅓ cup water to the pan and cover.
Steam for 5 minutes. Empty the pan
and wipe it dry between batches.

To make the dipping sauce, combine
all the ingredients in a small bowl.
Serve with the gyoza.

Makes 45

Honey shrimp

16 large shrimp
cornstarch, for dusting
vegetable oil, for deep-frying
3 egg whites, lightly beaten
2 tablespoons cornstarch, extra
2 tablespoons vegetable oil, extra
1/4 cup honey
2 tablespoons sesame seeds, toasted

Peel and devein the shrimp, leaving the tails intact. Pat them dry and lightly dust with the cornstarch, shaking off any excess. Fill a large, heavy-bottomed saucepan or wok one-third full of oil and heat to 350°F or until a cube of bread dropped in the oil browns in 15 seconds.

Beat the egg whites in a clean, dry bowl until soft peaks form. Add the extra cornstarch and some salt and gently whisk until combined and smooth. Using the tail as a handle, dip the shrimp in the batter, then slowly lower them into the oil. Cook in batches for 3–4 minutes or until crisp and golden and the shrimp are cooked. Remove with a slotted spoon, then drain on crumpled paper towels and keep warm.

Heat the extra oil and honey in a saucepan over medium heat for 2–3 minutes or until bubbling. Place the shrimp on a serving plate and pour on the honey sauce. Sprinkle with the sesame seeds and serve immediately with steamed rice.

Makes 16

Toasted figs in prosciutto

¼ cup unsalted butter
2 tablespoons orange juice
6 small/medium fresh figs
6 long, thin slices of prosciutto,
  trimmed of excess fat
24 sage leaves

Place the butter in a small, heavy-bottomed saucepan. Melt over low heat, then cook the butter for 8–10 minutes or until the froth subsides and the milk solids appear as brown specks on the bottom of the saucepan. Strain the butter into a clean bowl by pouring it through a strainer lined with a clean dishcloth or paper towel. Stir the orange juice into the strained butter.

Gently slice the figs lengthwise into quarters. Cut each slice of prosciutto into four even strips. Place a sage leaf on each fig segment, then wrap a piece of prosciutto around the middle with the ends tucked under the bottom of the fig. Arrange the figs, cut-side up, on a baking sheet and brush lightly with the butter mixture.

Move the broiler pan to its lowest position, then preheat the broiler to hot. Place the baking sheet of figs on the broiler pan and toast the figs for 1–1½ minutes or until the prosciutto becomes slightly crispy. Serve hot or at room temperature.

Makes 24

Think ahead: The figs can be wrapped up to 6 hours in advance and covered in plastic wrap. Cook them just before serving.

Zucchini and haloumi fritters

³/₄ lb. zucchini
4 scallions, thinly sliced
6 oz. haloumi cheese, coarsely grated
¹/₄ cup all-purpose flour
2 eggs
1 tablespoon chopped, fresh dill,
   plus sprigs, to garnish
¹/₄ cup vegetable oil
1 lemon, cut into very thin slices,
   seeds removed
¹/₃ cup plain yogurt

Coarsely grate the zucchini and squeeze out as much liquid as possible in your hands or in a clean dishcloth. Combine the zucchini with the scallions, haloumi, flour, eggs, and dill. Season well with salt and cracked black pepper.

Heat the oil in a large, heavy-bottomed frying pan. Form fritters (using heaping teaspoons of the mixture) and cook in batches for 2 minutes each side or until they are golden and firm. Drain on crumpled paper towels.

Cut each slice of lemon into quarters or eighths, depending on the size, to make small triangles.

Top each fritter with ¹/₂ teaspoon yogurt, a piece of lemon, and a small sprig of dill.

Makes 45

Note: The fritters are best prepared and cooked as close to the serving time as possible—otherwise the haloumi becomes a little tough.

Shrimp toasts

Dipping sauce
1/2 cup ketchup
2 cloves garlic, crushed
2 small, fresh red chilies, seeded and
  finely chopped
2 tablespoons hoisin sauce
2 teaspoons Worcestershire sauce

11 oz. medium shrimp
1 clove garlic
1/2 cup canned water chestnuts,
  drained
1 tablespoon chopped cilantro
3/4 x 3/4-inch piece fresh ginger,
  roughly chopped
2 eggs, separated
1/4 teaspoon white pepper
12 slices white bread, crusts removed
1 cup sesame seeds
vegetable oil, for deep-frying

To make the dipping sauce, combine
all the ingredients in a small bowl.

Peel the shrimp and gently pull out
the dark vein from each shrimp back,
starting at the head end. Put the
shrimp in a food processor with the
garlic, water chestnuts, cilantro,
ginger, egg whites, pepper, and
1/4 teaspoon salt, and process for
20–30 seconds or until smooth.

Brush the top of each slice of bread
with lightly beaten egg yolk, then
spread the shrimp mixture evenly.
Sprinkle generously with sesame
seeds. Cut each slice of bread into
three even strips.

Fill a large, heavy-bottomed saucepan
one-third full of oil and heat to 350°F
or until a cube of bread browns in
15 seconds. Deep-fry the toasts in
batches for 10–15 seconds or until
golden and crisp. Start with the
shrimp mixture facedown, then turn
halfway through. Remove the toasts
from the oil with tongs or a slotted
spoon and drain on crumpled paper
towels. Serve with the dipping sauce.

Makes 36

Think ahead: The uncooked shrimp
toasts can be frozen for up to
a month. Allow them to thaw slightly
before deep-frying as instructed.

Deep-fried chicken balls

2 oz. dried rice vermicelli
1 lb. ground chicken
3 cloves garlic, finely chopped
1 tablespoon chopped, fresh ginger
1 fresh red chili, seeded and finely
  chopped
1 egg, lightly beaten
2 scallions, finely sliced
1/3 cup chopped cilantro leaves
1/3 cup all-purpose flour
1/3 cup finely chopped water
  chestnuts
vegetable oil, for deep-frying

Dipping sauce
1/2 cup sweet chili sauce
1/2 cup soy sauce
1 tablespoon Chinese rice wine

Cover the vermicelli with boiling water and soak for 6–7 minutes. Drain, then cut into short pieces.

Combine the chicken, garlic, ginger, chili, egg, scallions, cilantro, flour, and water chestnuts in a large bowl. Mix in the vermicelli and season with salt. Refrigerate for 30 minutes. Roll heaping tablespoons of the mixture into small balls.

Fill a wok or deep saucepan one-third full with oil and heat to 350°F or until a cube of bread browns in 15 seconds. Deep-fry the balls in batches for 2 minutes or until golden brown and cooked through. Drain.

To make the dipping sauce, mix the sweet chili sauce, soy sauce, and rice wine. Serve with the hot chicken balls.

Makes about 30

Mushroom ragout tartlets

Basic pastry cases
2 cups all-purpose flour
½ cup chilled butter, chopped
1 egg

¼ cup butter
4 scallions, chopped
2 cloves garlic, chopped
1⅔ cups small portobello or shiitake
  mushrooms, thinly sliced
1 cup oyster mushrooms, cut into
  eighths
½ cup enoki mushrooms, trimmed,
  pulled apart, and sliced lengthwise
3 teaspoons all-purpose flour
2 tablespoons chicken stock or water
2 tablespoons sake
⅓ cup heavy whipping cream
snow pea sprouts, stems removed

Preheat the oven to 400°F. Lightly grease thirty mini muffin cups. Sift the flour and rub the butter in with your fingertips until the mixture resembles fine breadcrumbs. Make a hollow in the center, add the egg, and mix with a rubber spatula or palette knife, using a cutting action, until it comes together in beads. If the dough seems too dry, add a little cold water. Press the dough into a ball on a lightly floured surface, then wrap it in plastic wrap and refrigerate for 30 minutes.

Roll out the dough between sheets of baking parchment to ⅛ inch thick. Cut out thirty rounds with a 2½-inch cutter. Press a round into each cup. Prick the bottoms with a fork and bake for 8 minutes or until golden. If they puff up, use a clean cloth to press back. Allow to cool.

Melt the butter in a frying pan over medium heat, add the scallions and garlic, and cook for 1 minute. Add the mushrooms and cook, stirring, for 3–4 minutes or until soft. Add the flour and stir for another minute. Pour in the stock and sake, and stir for 1 minute or until evaporated. Then add the cream and cook for 1 minute or until thickened. Season. Spoon into the prepared pastry cases and top each one with a snow pea sprout leaf.

Makes 30

Tomato and basil bruschetta

1 loaf Italian bread
1 large clove garlic, peeled
extra-virgin olive oil, to drizzle
3 large, vine-ripened tomatoes, cut
   into 1/2-inch pieces
1/4 cup extra-virgin olive oil
1/3 cup fresh basil, torn into small
   pieces

Preheat the oven to 400°F. Slice the loaf of bread diagonally into twelve 1/2-inch-thick slices. Lay the bread slices out in a single layer on a baking sheet and bake for 10–12 minutes or until they are lightly golden. Remove from the oven and rub the garlic clove over one side of each slice of toast. Lightly drizzle each slice with extra-virgin olive oil, then cut them in half again.

Place the tomato slices in a bowl with the extra-virgin olive oil and torn basil. Season with salt and cracked black pepper and toss until well combined. Spoon the mixture onto the prepared bruschetta slices and serve immediately.

Makes 24

Note: Bruschetta are best made just before serving to keep the bread from drying out or the topping from making the bread soggy.
Variation: A simple alternative to topping is to lightly sprinkle the prepared bruschetta with some fresh or dried chopped herbs.

Scallops with goat cheese and crispy prosciutto

4 thin slices prosciutto
16 scallops in shells, roe and
   beards removed
2–3 tablespoons extra-virgin olive oil
1 tablespoon chopped, fresh
   Italian parsley
1/2 teaspoon sea salt flakes
3 1/2 oz. goat cheese, crumbled
2 tablespoons balsamic vinegar

Cook the prosciutto under a hot broiler until crisp, then drain on paper towels and break into small pieces.

Place the scallops on two baking sheets. Combine the oil and parsley in a small bowl and season with sea salt and cracked black pepper. Brush the scallops with the oil mixture.

Cook the scallops in batches under a hot broiler for 2–3 minutes or until they are tender.

Top the scallops with the goat's cheese, prosciutto, and a drizzle of balsamic vinegar.

Carefully transfer the scallops from the baking sheets to serving plates lined with rock salt—the shells will be very hot. Serve with small cocktail forks to make eating easier.

Makes 16

Corn pancakes

6 fresh ears of corn or 11-oz. can
   corn, drained
4 scallions, finely chopped
1 clove garlic, crushed
1 teaspoon curry powder
2 tablespoons self-rising flour
1 teaspoon soy sauce
1 egg
vegetable oil, for frying

If using fresh corn, remove the kernels with a sharp knife. Combine the corn, scallions, garlic, curry powder, flour, soy sauce, and egg, mashing lightly with a potato masher. Cover with plastic wrap and chill for 1 hour.

Heat 4 tablespoons of oil in a frying pan. Drop tablespoons of the corn mixture into the pan—try to avoid overcrowding. Cook over medium heat for 2–3 minutes on each side or until golden brown. Turn carefully to keep the pancakes from breaking. Remove from the pan and drain on paper towels. Repeat with the remaining mixture.

Delicious served with sweet chili sauce.

Makes 12

Sigara Boregi

1 lb. spinach
1 tablespoon olive oil
4 cloves garlic, crushed
8 shallots, finely chopped
½ cup crumbled feta
1 egg, lightly beaten
3 tablespoons chopped, fresh
  Italian parsley
¼ teaspoon finely grated lemon zest
¼ teaspoon paprika
pinch of nutmeg
6 sheets phyllo pastry
4 oz. butter, melted
extra-virgin olive oil, for deep-frying

Wash the spinach, leaving it fairly wet. Place in a saucepan, cover, and cook over low heat until just wilted. Transfer the spinach to a colander and press out the liquid with a wooden spoon. When cool, squeeze dry.

Heat the oil in a frying pan and cook the garlic and shallots for 2 minutes or until soft but not browned. Transfer to a bowl and add the feta, egg, parsley, spinach, and lemon zest. Season with the paprika, nutmeg, salt, and pepper, and mix well.

Brush a sheet of phyllo with melted butter, then fold it in half lengthwise. It should measure about 13 x 5 inches. Cut in half widthwise. Brush with butter, place 1 heaping tablespoon of filling at one end of each piece, and spread, leaving a ½-inch border on each side. Fold in the sides to cover the edges of the filling, continuing the folds right up the length of the pastry. Brush with melted butter, then roll up tightly. Brush the outside with butter and seal. Cover with a damp dishcloth while you prepare the rest.

Heat the extra-virgin olive oil in a deep frying pan to 350°F or until a cube of bread browns in 15 seconds. Deep-fry in batches until golden. Serve warm or at room temperature.

Makes 12

Crunchy Thai chicken and peanut cakes

3 teaspoons light brown sugar
1 tablespoon fish sauce
11 oz. ground chicken
3/4 cup toasted peanuts, chopped
1/2 cup fresh breadcrumbs
1 tablespoon red Thai curry paste
1 tablespoon lime juice
3 fresh kaffir lime leaves, very finely
  shredded
2 tablespoons sweet chili sauce
2 tablespoons chopped cilantro
1/2 cup vegetable oil
1 banana leaf, cut into 24
  2-inch squares
sweet chili sauce, extra, to serve

Dissolve the sugar in the fish sauce, then place in a bowl with the chicken, peanuts, breadcrumbs, curry paste, lime juice, lime leaves, sweet chili sauce, and cilantro. Mix well. Divide the mixture into twenty-four small balls—they will be quite soft. Flatten the balls into disks about 1/2 inch thick. Lay them in a single layer on a baking sheet, cover with plastic wrap, and refrigerate for 30 minutes.

Heat the oil in a heavy-bottomed frying pan and cook the cakes in batches for 2–3 minutes each side or until firm and golden. Drain on crumpled paper towels.

Place a chicken cake on each square of banana leaf and top with a dash of sweet chili sauce. Secure with a toothpick for easier serving.

Makes 24

Think ahead: The uncooked Thai chicken cakes will keep refrigerated, in a single layer, for 1 day or frozen for up to 2 months.

Grilled vegetable skewers

24 bay leaves
12 button mushrooms, cut in half
1 yellow pepper, cut into 3/4-inch
  pieces
1 red pepper, cut into 3/4-inch pieces
1 zucchini, cut into 3/4-inch pieces
1 small red onion, cut into 3/4-inch
  pieces
1/2 cup olive oil
2 tablespoons lemon juice
1 clove garlic, crushed
2 teaspoons fresh thyme

Concassé
1 tablespoon olive oil
1 small onion, finely chopped
1 clove garlic, crushed
14-oz. can diced tomatoes
4 tablespoons torn, fresh basil

Thread twenty-four skewers in the following order: bay leaf, mushroom, yellow pepper, red pepper, zucchini, and onion, then put in a large, flat, nonmetallic dish and season with salt and cracked black pepper.

Place the oil, lemon juice, garlic, and thyme in a small bowl and mix together. Pour over the skewers and marinate for 20 minutes.

Meanwhile, to make the concassé, heat the oil in a small saucepan, add the onion, and cook for 5 minutes or until soft. Add the garlic and cook for 30 seconds, then add the tomatoes. Simmer for 10–15 minutes over medium heat, then add the basil. Barbecue the skewers or cook on a hot, ridged grill pan for 3 minutes each side or until golden, brushing occasionally with the marinade. Serve with the concassé.

Makes 24

Salt cod fritters

1 lb. salt cod
1 large potato, unpeeled
2 tablespoons milk
¼ cup olive oil
1 small onion, finely chopped
2 cloves garlic, crushed
¼ cup self-rising flour
2 eggs, separated
1 tablespoon finely chopped, fresh
 Italian parsley
vegetable oil, for deep-frying

Soak the cod in cold water for 24 hours, changing the water at least three times. Boil the potato for 20 minutes or until soft. Drain. When cool enough to handle, peel and mash with the milk and 2 tablespoons of the olive oil. Drain the cod, cut into pieces, and place in a saucepan. Cover with cold water, bring to a boil, then simmer for 10 minutes or until soft. Drain. When cool enough to handle, remove the skin and any bones. Mash with a fork until flaky. (You should have 6½ oz. of flesh.)

Heat the remaining olive oil in a frying pan. Cook the onion over medium heat for 5 minutes or until softened and turning brown. Add the garlic and cook for 1 minute. Remove the pan from the heat.

Combine the potato, cod, onion mixture, flour, egg yolks, and parsley, and season with cracked black pepper. Whisk the egg whites until stiff, then fold into the mixture.

Fill a large, heavy-bottomed saucepan one-third full of oil and heat to 375°F or until a cube of bread browns in 10 seconds. Drop level tablespoons of the mixture into the oil and cook for 2 minutes or until puffed and golden. Drain on paper towels and serve.

Makes 28

Shrimp in Chinese pancakes

24 medium shrimp, peeled and
  deveined
$\frac{1}{3}$ cup Chinese rice wine
  or dry sherry
2 tablespoons soy sauce
2 teaspoons sesame oil
2 tablespoons vegetable oil
4 cloves garlic, finely chopped
$\frac{1}{2}$ x 1$\frac{1}{2}$-inch piece fresh ginger,
  peeled and finely shredded
$\frac{1}{2}$–$\frac{2}{3}$ cup Chinese plum sauce
2 teaspoons chili sauce
2 scallions, finely chopped
24 Chinese pancakes (see Note)
1 small cucumber, peeled, seeded,
  and cut into thin, 2-inch-long strips
12 garlic chives, cut into 2-inch
  pieces

Place the shrimp in a nonmetallic
bowl with the rice wine, soy sauce,
and sesame oil, and marinate for at
least 10 minutes.

Heat a wok over high heat, add the
vegetable oil, and swirl to coat. Add
the garlic and ginger, and sauté for
1–2 minutes. Use a slotted spoon or
tongs to remove the shrimp from the
marinade and add them to the wok.
Save the marinade. Stir the shrimp for
2 minutes or until they start to turn
pink, then add the plum sauce, chili
sauce, and the reserved marinade.
Stir-fry for 2–3 minutes or until the
shrimp are cooked, curled, and
slightly glazed. Remove from the heat
and stir in the scallions.

Place the pancakes in a nonstick
frying pan over medium heat for
1 minute or until warm.

To assemble, put a shrimp, a few
slices of cucumber, and a few chive
pieces on each pancake, spoon
on some sauce, then fold over.
Serve immediately.

Makes 24

Note: The pancakes, traditionally
used for Peking duck, can be found in
the freezer section of Asian markets.

Spring rolls

2 oz. mung bean vermicelli
1 tablespoon vegetable oil
2 large cloves garlic, crushed
2 tablespoons grated, fresh ginger
6 scallions, chopped
4 cilantro roots, finely chopped
6½ oz. peeled shrimp, minced
6½ oz. ground pork
1 carrot (¼ lb.), grated
3 tablespoons finely chopped
    cilantro leaves
2 tablespoons sweet chili sauce
1 tablespoon fish sauce
2 tablespoons soy sauce
30 small spring roll wrappers
1 egg white, lightly beaten
vegetable oil, extra, for deep-frying

Soak the vermicelli in warm water for 5 minutes. Drain and cut into short pieces.

Heat the oil in a large saucepan over medium heat. Add the garlic, ginger, scallions, and cilantro roots. Cook for 1–2 minutes or until soft. Add the shrimp and ground pork and cook until done, breaking up the lumps. Stir in the vermicelli, carrot, and cilantro leaves. Cook for 1 minute. Add the sweet chili, fish, and soy sauces and cook for 2 minutes or until dry. Allow to cool.

Place a tablespoon of the mixture along the center of each spring roll wrapper. Brush the edge with egg white and roll up, tucking in the ends as you go. Cover to keep from drying out.

Fill a deep, heavy-bottomed saucepan one-third full of oil and heat to 375°F or until a cube of bread browns in 10 seconds. Cook the rolls, in batches, for 30–60 seconds or until golden. Drain well before serving.

Makes 30

Sesame and wasabi-crusted tuna cubes

Ginger and soy dipping sauce
3/4 x 3/4-inch piece fresh ginger, julienned
2 tablespoons Japanese soy sauce
2 tablespoons mirin
1 teaspoon wasabi paste
1/4 teaspoon sesame oil

Tuna cubes
1 1/4 lbs. fresh tuna steaks
1 teaspoon wasabi powder
1/3 cup black sesame seeds
1/4 cup vegetable oil

To make the dipping sauce, combine the ginger, Japanese soy sauce, mirin, wasabi paste, and sesame oil.

Cut the tuna into 3/4-inch cubes using a very sharp knife. Toss with the combined wasabi powder and black sesame seeds until evenly coated.

Heat a wok over high heat, add half the oil, and swirl to coat. Add half the tuna and cook, tossing gently, for 1–2 minutes or until lightly golden on the outside but still pink in the middle. Drain on crumpled paper towels and repeat with the remaining oil and tuna. Arrange on a platter with dipping sauce in the center and serve with toothpicks so that your guests can pick up the cubes.

Makes about 40

Think ahead: The dipping sauce will keep in the refrigerator for up to a week, but the tuna is best if cooked no more than 3 hours in advance. Variation: Try a chili and lime dipping sauce instead of the ginger and soy one used in this recipe. Dissolve 2 tablespoons light brown sugar in 2 tablespoons lime juice. Add 1 tablespoon fish sauce and 1 seeded, chopped, fresh bird's-eye chili. Mix together well. This sauce will keep in the refrigerator for 2–3 days.

Pesto palmiers

1 cup fresh basil leaves
1 clove garlic, crushed
¼ cup grated Parmesan
1 tablespoon pine nuts, toasted
2 tablespoons olive oil
4 sheets frozen puff pastry, thawed

Preheat the oven to 425°F. Roughly chop the basil leaves in a food processor with the garlic, Parmesan, and pine nuts. While processing, gradually add the oil and process until the mixture is smooth.

Spread each pastry sheet with a quarter of the basil mixture. Roll up one side until you reach the middle, then repeat with the other side. Place on a baking sheet. Repeat with the remaining pastry and basil mixture. Freeze for 30 minutes.

Slice each roll into ½-inch slices. Curl each slice into a semicircle and place on a lightly greased baking sheet. Allow room for the palmiers to expand during cooking. Bake in batches for 15–20 minutes or until golden brown.

Makes 60

Note: Traditionally made sweet, palmiers are delicious, bite-size, pastry snacks.
Variations: Spread with a prepared tapenade paste made with olives, capers, anchovies, oil, and garlic, or with tahini, a sesame seed paste. Another simple version is to sprinkle just the grated Parmesan between the pastry layers.

Shrimp, noodle, and nori packets

Dipping sauce
1/3 cup tonkatsu sauce or barbecue
  sauce
2 tablespoons lemon juice
1 tablespoon sake or mirin
1–2 teaspoons grated, fresh ginger

8 oz. dried somen noodles
3 sheets nori (dried seaweed)
1/2 cup all-purpose flour
2 egg yolks
24 medium shrimp, peeled and
  deveined, with the tails intact
vegetable oil, for deep-frying

Combine the dipping sauce ingredients, adding the ginger to taste.

Using a sharp knife, cut the noodles to the same length as the shrimp (from the head to the base of the tail). Keep the noodles in neat bundles. Cut the nori into 1-inch-wide strips.

Sift the flour and make a hollow in the center. Mix the egg yolks with 1/4 cup of water. Gradually add to the flour, whisking to make a smooth batter. Add another tablespoon of water if the mixture is too thick.

Dip a shrimp in the batter, letting the excess run off. Roll the shrimp lengthwise in noodles to coat it with a single layer. Keep the noodles in place by rolling a nori strip around the center of the shrimp and securing it with a little batter. Repeat with the rest of the shrimp.

Fill a deep, heavy-bottomed pan or deep-fryer one-third full of oil and heat to 350°F or until a cube of bread browns in 15 seconds. Deep-fry 2–3 shrimp at a time for 1–2 minutes or until the shrimp are cooked. Drain on crumpled paper towels. Serve warm with the dipping sauce.

Makes 24

Dressed-up baby potatoes

24 bite-size new potatoes, washed
  and dried
1/3 cup olive oil
1 tablespoon drained capers,
  patted dry
1 slice bacon
1 tablespoon whipping cream
1/2 tablespoon butter
1/2 cup sour cream
1 tablespoon chopped, fresh chives
1 tablespoon red or black caviar

Preheat the oven to 350°F. Line a baking sheet with baking parchment. Place the potatoes in a bowl and toss with half the olive oil. Sprinkle with salt and black pepper, then put on the baking sheet and bake for 40 minutes or until cooked through, rotating them 2–3 times so that they brown evenly.

Meanwhile, heat the remaining oil in a frying pan and cook the capers over high heat or until they open into small flowers. Drain on paper towels. Cook the bacon under a hot broiler until crispy. Cool, then chop finely.

Remove the potatoes from the oven. When cool enough to handle, cut a thin lid from each potato. Discard the lids. Use a melon baller or small teaspoon to scoop out the flesh from the middle of the potatoes, leaving a 1/2-inch border. Put the potato flesh in a bowl and mash thoroughly with the cream, butter, salt, and black pepper. Spoon the mixture back into the potatoes.

Top each potato with a small dollop of sour cream. Divide the potatoes into four groups of six and use a separate topping for each group: capers, bacon, chives, and caviar.

Makes 24

Moneybags

1 tablespoon peanut oil
4 red Asian shallots, finely chopped
2 cloves garlic, crushed
1 tablespoon grated, fresh ginger
5 oz. ground chicken
5 oz. ground pork
¼ cup roasted peanuts, chopped
3 tablespoons finely chopped
  cilantro leaves
3 teaspoons fish sauce
2 teaspoons soy sauce
2 teaspoons lime juice
2 teaspoons light brown sugar
30 wonton wrappers
vegetable oil, for deep-frying
garlic chives, for tying

Dipping sauce
2 teaspoons sugar
½ cup vinegar
2 small, fresh red chilies, seeded and
  chopped

Heat the oil in a frying pan over medium heat. Add the shallots, garlic, and ginger, and cook for 1–2 minutes or until the shallots are soft. Add the meat and cook for 4 minutes or until cooked, breaking up any lumps with a wooden spoon. Stir in the peanuts, cilantro, fish sauce, soy sauce, lime juice, and sugar, and cook, stirring, for 1–2 minutes or until mixed and reduced. Cool.

Form your thumb and index finger into a circle, and place a wonton wrapper on top. Place 2 teaspoons of the cooled mixture in the center, then lightly brush the edges with water. Push the mixture down firmly with your free hand, tightening the circle of your thumb and index finger at the same time, encasing the mixture in the wrapper and forming a bag. Trim.

Fill a deep, heavy-bottomed saucepan or deep-fryer one-third full of oil and heat to 375°F or until a cube of bread browns in 10 seconds. Cook in batches for 30–60 seconds or until golden. Drain. Tie the neck of the moneybags with the chives.

To make the dipping sauce, dissolve the sugar and 1 teaspoon salt in the vinegar. Add the chilies and mix. Serve with the dipping sauce.

Makes 30

Cocktail leek pies

¼ cup butter
2 tablespoons olive oil
1 onion, finely chopped
3 leeks, finely sliced
1 clove garlic, chopped
1 tablespoon all-purpose flour
2 tablespoons sour cream
1 cup grated Parmesan
1 teaspoon chopped, fresh thyme
4 sheets frozen puff pastry, thawed
1 egg, lightly beaten

Heat the butter and oil in a large frying pan over medium heat. Add the onion and cook, stirring occasionally, for 2 minutes. Add the leeks and garlic and cook for 5 minutes or until the leeks are softened and lightly browned. Add the flour and stir into the mixture for 1 minute. Add the sour cream and stir until slightly thickened. Transfer to a bowl and add the Parmesan and thyme. Season with salt and cracked black pepper and allow to cool.

Preheat the oven to 400°F. Place a lightly greased baking sheet in the oven to heat. Using a 2½-inch cutter, cut the pastry into sixty-four circles. Place 2 heaping teaspoons of filling on half the pastry circles, leaving a small border. Lightly brush the edges with egg, then place a pastry circle on top of each. Seal the edges well with a fork. Lightly brush the tops with egg. Place the pies on the heated sheet and bake for 25 minutes or until the pies are puffed and golden.

Makes 32

Mini focaccia with roasted vegetables

2 red peppers
2 yellow peppers
3 slender eggplants
2 large zucchini
1 red onion
1/3 cup extra-virgin olive oil
3 cloves garlic, crushed
12 mini focaccias, halved
1/4 cup pesto
3 large bocconcini (fresh mozzarella), sliced

Preheat the oven to 400°F. Cut the red and yellow peppers into 1 1/4-inch pieces. Slice the eggplants and zucchini into 1/2-inch rounds, then thinly slice the onion. Place all the vegetables in a roasting pan with the oil and garlic, season with salt and cracked black pepper, and toss together thoroughly. Roast for 25 minutes or until cooked.

Spread each half of focaccia with 1/2 teaspoon of the pesto and divide the vegetables among them. Place two slices of bocconcini on top of each base, then top with the lid. Toast the focaccias on both sides on a hot ridged pan until heated through.

Slice each focaccia in half, then wrap a 1 1/4-inch-wide band of double baking parchment around the middle of the sandwiches and secure with string. Serve warm.

Makes 24

Ratatouille pies

¼ cup olive oil
1 eggplant, diced
1 onion, finely chopped
1 red pepper, diced
1 small zucchini, diced
1 tablespoon tomato paste
1 cup chopped tomatoes
1 teaspoon dried Italian herbs
1½-lb. pie pastry
1 egg, lightly beaten
pesto, to serve

Heat 2 tablespoons of the oil in a frying pan and cook the eggplant until golden. Remove from the pan. Heat the remaining oil in the pan, add the onion, pepper, and zucchini, and cook for 2 minutes. Stir in the tomato paste, fresh tomatoes, herbs, and eggplant. Cook for 20 minutes or until reduced. Allow to cool.

Meanwhile, preheat the oven to 350°F and put a baking sheet in the oven. Grease twenty-four small muffin cups. Roll the pastry thinly and cut out twenty-four rounds with a 2¾-inch cutter. Repeat with a 2¼-inch cutter. Put one of the larger rounds in each muffin cup and fill with the cooled filling. Dampen the edges of the small rounds and place them on top of the filling to seal the pies. Brush with egg. Put the muffin pan on the hot baking sheet and cook for 25 minutes or until golden. Cool slightly, then remove from the pan. Serve with pesto.

Makes 24

Mini crab cakes with cilantro paste

1 tablespoon butter
4 scallions, thinly sliced
1 egg
2 tablespoons sour cream
11 oz. fresh, white crabmeat, excess
  liquid squeezed out
1 small yellow pepper, finely diced
2 teaspoons chopped, fresh thyme
2½ cups fresh, white breadcrumbs
olive oil, for frying

Cilantro paste
1 clove garlic
1 green chili, seeded
½ teaspoon ground cumin
¼ teaspoon sugar
¾ cup cilantro leaves
½ cup fresh mint
1 tablespoon lemon juice
1½ tablespoons coconut cream
½ avocado

Line a baking sheet with baking parchment. Melt the butter in a frying pan over low heat. When it begins to foam, add the scallions and cook for 2 minutes or until softened. Remove from the heat and allow to cool.

Mix the egg and sour cream until just smooth. Add the scallions, crab, pepper, thyme, and ½ cup of the breadcrumbs. Season and mix together. Shape the mixture into flat rounds, using 1 level tablespoon for each. Place on the baking sheet and refrigerate for 30 minutes.

Meanwhile, to make the cilantro paste, process the garlic, chili, cumin, sugar, cilantro, mint, lemon juice, and ¼ teaspoon salt in a food processor until a fine paste forms. Add the coconut cream and continue to blend until smooth. Add the avocado, and using the pulse action, process until just smooth. Transfer to a bowl, cover with plastic wrap, and chill.

Using your hands, coat the crab cakes in the remaining breadcrumbs. Heat enough olive oil in a nonstick frying pan to just coat the bottom. Cook in batches for 2–3 minutes each side or until golden. Drain and serve warm with ½ teaspoon of cilantro paste on each.

Makes 24

Thai chicken balls

2 lbs. ground chicken
1 cup fresh breadcrumbs
4 scallions, sliced
1 tablespoon ground coriander
1 cup chopped cilantro
3 tablespoons sweet chili sauce
1–2 tablespoons lemon juice
vegetable oil, for frying

Preheat the oven to 400°F. Mix the chicken and breadcrumbs in a bowl.

Add the scallions, coriander, cilantro, chili sauce, and lemon juice, and mix well. Using damp hands, form the mixture into evenly shaped balls that are either small enough to eat with your fingers or large enough to use as burgers.

Heat the oil in a deep frying pan, and fry the chicken balls in batches over high heat until browned all over. Place them on a baking sheet and bake until cooked through. (Small chicken balls will take 5 minutes to cook, while larger ones will take 10–15 minutes.) The mixture makes a delicious filling for sausage rolls.

Serves 6

Lamb korma on mini pappadums

11-oz. lamb fillet, cut into $1/2$-inch cubes
2 tablespoons korma curry paste
1 clove garlic, crushed
1 teaspoon ground coriander
$1/2$ cup plain yogurt
vegetable oil, for deep-frying
24 round $1 1/2$-inch pappadums (chili flavor, if available)
1 tablespoon vegetable oil, extra
$1 1/2$ tablespoons mango chutney
small cilantro leaves, to garnish

Combine the lamb, curry paste, garlic, ground coriander, and half the yogurt in a nonmetallic bowl. Cover and refrigerate for 1–2 hours.

Meanwhile, fill a deep, heavy-bottomed saucepan or deep-fryer one-third full of oil and heat to 350°F or until a cube of bread browns in 15 seconds. Cook the pappadums a few at a time for a few seconds each or until they are puffed and lightly golden. Remove with a slotted spoon and drain on crumpled paper towels.

Heat a wok over high heat, add the extra oil, and swirl to coat. Add the marinated lamb and cook in batches, stirring, for 4–5 minutes or until the lamb is cooked through. Spoon a heaping teaspoon onto each pappadum and top with $1/2$ teaspoon of the remaining yogurt, then $1/4$ teaspoon of the chutney. Garnish with a cilantro leaf and serve immediately.

Makes 24

Think ahead: Lamb korma can be cooked and frozen for up to 2 months or refrigerated for 2–3 days. Reheat in a saucepan over low heat until warm.Variations: You can make chicken korma by replacing the lamb with 11 oz. diced chicken breasts.

Mini hamburgers

8 hamburger buns, split in half
13 oz. ground beef
¼ cup dry breadcrumbs
3 shallots, very finely chopped
1 tablespoon Dijon mustard
1 tablespoon Worcestershire sauce
⅓ cup ketchup
olive oil, for frying
3½ oz. thinly sliced cheddar, cut into
  24 1¼-inch squares
24 baby arugula leaves, stems
  removed and torn into 1-inch pieces
12 cornichons (baby gherkins), cut
  into thin slices

Stamp out rounds from the burger buns using a 1½-inch cutter; you should get twenty-four from the tops and twenty-four from the bottoms. If the buns are thick, trim them with a serrated knife after cutting them.

Combine the ground beef, breadcrumbs, chopped shallots, mustard, Worcestershire sauce, 1 tablespoon of the ketchup, salt, and cracked black pepper in a bowl. Divide the mixture into twenty-four walnut-size pieces. With wet hands, form them into patties.

Heat a large, heavy-bottomed frying pan with enough oil to just cover the bottom of the pan, and cook the patties over medium heat for 1 minute on each side or until browned, then place on a baking sheet.

Preheat the broiler and lightly toast both halves of the mini hamburger buns. Top each patty with a small slice of cheese and toast for 1 minute or until the cheese just starts to melt.

Place the patties on the bottom halves of the buns. Top with the arugula, cornichon, and the remaining ketchup. Gently press on the top half of the bun and secure with a toothpick. Serve warm.

Makes 24

Vegetable samosas

2 tablespoons vegetable oil
1 small onion, diced
1 tablespoon hot curry paste
1/2 lb. potatoes, cut into 1/2-inch cubes
1/4 lb. orange sweet potatoes, peeled
  and cut into 1/2-inch cubes
1 tablespoon light brown sugar
1/2 cup frozen peas
1/3 cup salted, roasted cashew nuts,
  chopped
1/2 cup roughly chopped cilantro
  leaves
2 lbs. (5 sheets) pie pastry
vegetable oil, for deep-frying

Dipping sauce
2 cups Greek yogurt
1 cup cilantro leaves, roughly
  chopped
1 teaspoon ground cumin

Heat the oil in a large, heavy-bottomed saucepan over medium heat. Cook the onion and hot curry paste for 5 minutes, stirring regularly until the mixture is fragrant and the onion is golden. Add the potatoes, orange sweet potatoes, and sugar. Cook, stirring regularly, for 10 minutes or until the potatoes are tender. Stir in the peas, reduce the heat to low, cover, and cook for another 5 minutes. If the mixture is sticking, add 1–2 tablespoons of water. Cool to room temperature.

To make the dipping sauce, combine all the ingredients in a bowl and chill until needed.

Season the vegetable mixture, then add the cashews and cilantro. Using a 2³⁄₄-inch cutter, cut nine circles from each sheet of pastry. Place 1 rounded teaspoon of filling in the middle of each circle. Fold the pastry over and pinch the sides together.

Fill a deep, heavy-bottomed saucepan one-third full of oil and heat to 325°F or until a cube of bread browns in 20 seconds. Deep-fry four samosas at a time for 3 minutes or until crisp and the pastry has "blistered" a little. Drain on paper towels. Serve warm with the dipping sauce.

Makes 45

Mini eggs Florentine

Hollandaise sauce
3 egg yolks
2 tablespoons lime or lemon juice
½ cup butter, melted

6–8 slices bread
vegetable oil spray
24 quail eggs
½ lb. spinach, trimmed

Preheat the oven to 350°F. To make the hollandaise sauce, blend the yolks and juice in a food processor for 5 seconds, then gradually add the melted butter. Transfer to a bowl and refrigerate for 30 minutes or until thickened.

Cut twenty-four rounds of bread with a 1½-inch cutter. Place on a baking sheet, spray with oil, and bake for 10 minutes. Turn over and bake for another 5 minutes, until dry and crisp.

Put about 1 inch of water in a large, nonstick frying pan and bring to a simmer. Reduce the heat so the water is not moving. Carefully crack the eggs into the water. Spoon a little water onto the top of the eggs as they cook, and when set, remove and drain on paper towels.

Steam or microwave the spinach for 2 minutes or until wilted, then drain well. To assemble, put some spinach on the bread rounds, then top with an egg and drizzle with hollandaise. Serve immediately.

Makes 24

Note: Look for quail eggs in specialty food stores. You can also use store-bought hollandaise.

Turkish pizza

Basic pizza dough
1 1/2 packets active dry yeast
1 teaspoon superfine sugar
4 cups all-purpose flour
2 tablespoons olive oil

1 tablespoon olive oil, plus extra
  for brushing
12 oz. ground lamb
1 onion, finely chopped
1/4 cup pine nuts
1 tomato, peeled, seeded, and
  chopped
1/4 teaspoon ground cinnamon
pinch of allspice
2 teaspoons chopped cilantro,
  plus extra for serving
2 teaspoons lemon juice
1/4 cup plain yogurt

Combine the yeast, sugar, and 3/4 cup warm water. Cover and leave for 10 minutes. If it hasn't foamed after 10 minutes, discard and start again.

Sift the flour and 1/2 teaspoon salt and make a hollow. Add the yeast mixture and oil. Mix with a rubber spatula or palette knife, using a cutting action, until a dough forms. Knead for 10 minutes or until smooth. Place in an oiled bowl, cover with plastic wrap, and leave for 45 minutes or until doubled in size.

Heat the oil in a frying pan over medium heat and cook the lamb for 3 minutes or until browned. Add the onion and cook over low heat for 8 minutes or until soft. Add the pine nuts, tomato, spices, 1/4 teaspoon cracked pepper, and some salt. Cook for 8 minutes or until dry. Stir in the cilantro and lemon juice, and season.

Preheat the oven to 450°F. Punch down the dough, then knead for 8 minutes or until elastic. Roll out into twenty-four ovals. Spoon some filling onto each base. Pinch together the two short sides to form a boat shape. Brush with oil, then place the pizzas on a greased baking sheet. Bake for 10 minutes. Serve with a dab of yogurt and some cilantro.

Makes 24

Olive and potato balls with pesto

1¼ lbs. russet potatoes
1 tablespoon olive oil
1 onion, finely chopped
2 cloves garlic, finely chopped
½ cup pitted Kalamata olives, sliced
⅓ cup all-purpose flour
¼ cup grated Parmesan
¼ cup shredded, fresh basil
1 egg
¾ cup dry Japanese breadcrumbs
  (see Note)
vegetable oil, for deep-frying
¼ cup pesto
2 slices prosciutto, sliced into
  thin strips

Cut the potatoes into 1½-inch chunks and steam or boil for 15 minutes or until tender. Drain well, then mash.

Heat the olive oil in a frying pan and cook the onion over medium heat for 4–5 minutes or until soft. Add the garlic and cook for an extra minute. Remove from the heat, cool, and add to the potatoes. Mix in the olives, flour, Parmesan, basil, egg, and a little salt and cracked black pepper. Shape the mixture into thirty small balls, then refrigerate for 30 minutes. Roll the balls in breadcrumbs, pressing the breadcrumbs on firmly so that the balls are evenly coated.

Fill a deep, heavy-bottomed saucepan or deep-fryer one-third full of oil and heat to 350°F or until a cube of bread browns in 15 seconds. Cook the olive and potato balls in batches for 2–3 minutes or until golden. Drain on crumpled paper towels. Top each with ½ teaspoon of the pesto and a piece of prosciutto.

Makes 30

Note: Japanese breadcrumbs provide a crispy coating, but you can also use regular breadcrumbs.
Think ahead: The balls can be frozen for up to 2 months before cooking or refrigerated for 2 days.

Lemongrass shrimp

6 lemongrass stalks, cut in half
   lengthwise, then in half crosswise
2 lbs. peeled and deveined shrimp
3 scallions, roughly chopped
4 tablespoons cilantro leaves
2 tablespoons fresh mint
2 tablespoons fish sauce
1½ tablespoons lime juice
1–2 tablespoons sweet chili sauce,
   plus extra for serving
peanut oil, for brushing

Soak the lemongrass in water for 30 minutes, then pat dry. Process the shrimp, scallions, cilantro, mint, fish sauce, lime juice, and chili sauce in a food processor. Mold a tablespoon of the mix around the end of a lemongrass stalk, using wet hands. Refrigerate for 30 minutes.

Brush a ridged grill pan with the oil. Cook the skewers, turning occasionally, for 5 minutes or until cooked. Serve with sweet chili sauce.

Makes 24

Empanadas

2 eggs
¼ cup stuffed green olives, chopped
3 oz. ham, finely chopped
¼ cup grated cheddar
3 sheets frozen puff pastry, thawed
1 egg yolk, lightly beaten

Place the eggs in a small saucepan, cover with water, and bring to a boil. Boil for 10 minutes, then drain and cool for 5 minutes in cold water. Peel and chop.

Preheat the oven to 425°F. Lightly grease two baking sheets. Combine the eggs, olives, ham, and cheddar in a large bowl.

Cut five 4-inch rounds from each pastry sheet. Place a tablespoon of the filling into the center of each round, fold the pastry over, and crimp the edges to seal.

Place the pastries on the sheets, about ¾ inch apart. Brush with the egg yolk and bake in the center or top half of the oven for 15 minutes or until well browned and puffed. Swap the sheets around after 10 minutes and cover loosely with aluminum foil if the empanadas start to brown too much. Serve hot.

Makes 15

Moroccan lamb pies

Filling

2 tablespoons olive oil

1 onion, thinly sliced

2 cloves garlic, crushed

2 teaspoons ground cumin

2 teaspoons ground ginger

2 teaspoons paprika

1 teaspoon ground turmeric

1 teaspoon ground cinnamon

1-lb. lamb fillet, diced

1½ cups beef stock

1 tablespoon finely chopped, preserved lemon

2 tablespoons sliced Kalamata olives

1 tablespoon chopped cilantro

24 pastry shells

1½-lb. pie pastry

1 egg, lightly beaten

Heat the oil in a large saucepan over medium heat, then add the onion, garlic, and spices. Add the lamb to the saucepan and coat in the spice mixture. Pour in the stock, cover, and cook over low heat for 30 minutes. Add the lemon and cook, uncovered, for another 20 minutes or until the liquid has reduced and the lamb is tender. Stir in the olives and cilantro and allow to cool.

Meanwhile, heat the oven to 350°F and put a baking sheet in the oven. Grease twenty-four small muffin cups. Roll the pastry thinly and cut out twenty-four rounds with a 2¾-inch cutter. Repeat with a 2¼-inch cutter. Put one of the larger rounds in each muffin cup and fill with the cooled filling. Dampen the edges of the small rounds and place them on top of the filling to seal the pies. Brush with the egg. Put the pan on the hot baking tray and cook for 25 minutes or until golden. Cool slightly, then remove from the pan. Delicious served with a dollop of plain yogurt.

Makes 24

Peking duck rolls

1 cup all-purpose flour
1/2 teaspoon sesame oil
1/2 large Chinese roast duck
6 scallions, cut into 2 1/2-inch pieces
  (24 pieces total)
1 small cucumber, seeded and cut
  into 2 1/2 x 1/4-inch slices
2–3 tablespoons hoisin sauce
2 teaspoons toasted sesame seeds
24 chives, blanched

Sift the flour, make a hollow in the center, and pour in the sesame oil and 1/2 cup boiling water. Stir until the mixture forms a slightly sticky, soft dough. Add a few teaspoons of boiling water if needed. Knead on a floured surface for 5 minutes or until smooth. Cover and let rest for 10 minutes.

Shred the duck into pieces and cut the skin into small strips.

Divide the dough into twenty-four pieces, then roll each piece into a 3-inch round on a floured board. Cover with plastic wrap while you are working to keep the dough from drying out.

Heat a nonstick frying pan over medium-high heat and dry-fry the pancakes for 20 seconds each side. Do not overcook or they will become too crispy for rolling. Stack on a plate and keep warm. If necessary, reheat by microwaving on high for 20 seconds or wrapping in foil and baking in a 325°F oven until warm.

Arrange a piece of scallion, cucumber, duck flesh, and skin on a pancake. Add 1/2 teaspoon hoisin and sprinkle with sesame seeds. Roll firmly and tie with a chive.

Makes 24

Goat cheese fritters with roasted pepper sauce

Roasted pepper sauce
2 red peppers
2 tablespoons olive oil
1 small red onion, finely chopped
1 clove garlic
1/3 cup chicken or vegetable stock

1 2/3 cups ricotta, well drained
13 oz. goat cheese, crumbled
2 tablespoons chopped, fresh chives
1/4 cup all-purpose flour
2 eggs, lightly beaten
1 cup dry breadcrumbs
vegetable oil, for deep-frying

Cut the peppers into 2–3 pieces, removing the seeds and membrane. Place, skin-side up, under a hot broiler until the skin blackens and blisters. Cool in a plastic bag, then peel the skin and chop the flesh.

Heat the olive oil in a frying pan over medium heat, and cook the onion and garlic for 5 minutes or until softened. Add the peppers and stock. Bring to a boil, then remove from the heat, cool slightly, and transfer to a food processor. Pulse until combined but still a little lumpy. Season and refrigerate until needed.

Combine the ricotta, goat cheese, and chives in a bowl. Add the flour and eggs, then season and mix well.

Put the breadcrumbs in a bowl. Roll a tablespoon of the cheese mixture into a ball with damp hands, flatten slightly, and coat in the breadcrumbs. Repeat with the remaining mixture. Refrigerate for 30 minutes.

Fill a deep, heavy-bottomed saucepan one-third full of oil and heat to 350°F or until a cube of bread browns in 15 seconds. Cook in batches for 1 minute or until browned, then drain. Serve warm with the pepper sauce.

Makes 30

Tofu and vegetable koftas with yogurt dipping sauce

Yogurt dipping sauce
3/4 cup plain yogurt
1 clove garlic, crushed
2 tablespoons fresh mint, finely
  chopped

8-oz. firm tofu
4 tablespoons olive oil
1 1/2 cups grated butternut squash
  (see Note)
3/4 cup grated zucchini (see Note)
1 onion, chopped
4 cloves garlic, crushed
4 small scallions, finely chopped
1/4 cup chopped cilantro leaves
1 tablespoon Madras curry powder
1 cup whole-wheat flour
1/2 cup grated Parmesan
vegetable oil, for deep-frying

To make the dipping sauce, place the yogurt, garlic, and mint in a bowl, season, and mix together well. Add a little water, if needed.

Blend the tofu in a food processor or blender until finely processed.

Heat the olive oil in a frying pan. Add the pumpkin, zucchini, onion, and garlic, and cook over medium heat, stirring occasionally, for 10 minutes or until the vegetables are tender. Cool.

Add the scallions, cilantro, curry powder, 1/2 cup of the whole-wheat flour, Parmesan, tofu, and 1 tablespoon salt, and mix well. Roll a tablespoon of the mixture between your hands to form a ball, then repeat with the remaining mixture. Coat the balls in the remaining flour.

Fill a deep, heavy-bottomed pan one-third full of oil and heat to 350°F or until a cube of bread browns in 15 seconds. Cook the tofu and vegetable koftas in small batches for 2–3 minutes or until golden brown. Drain on paper towels. Serve with the dipping sauce.

Serves 4

Note: When buying the vegetables, buy a 3/4-lb. butternut squash and a 6-oz. zucchini.

Grilled shrimp with tequila mayonnaise

24 jumbo shrimp
1/3 cup olive oil
2 tablespoons lime juice
1 tablespoon tequila
2/3 cup mayonnaise

Peel and devein the shrimp, keeping the tails intact. Combine the olive oil with the lime juice in a nonmetallic bowl and season with salt and cracked black pepper. Add the shrimp, cover, and leave to marinate for 1 hour. Meanwhile, mix the tequila into the mayonnaise, then transfer to a serving dish.

Heat a ridged grill pan until hot, add the shrimp, and cook for 1–2 minutes on each side until pink and cooked through. Serve with the tequila mayonnaise for dipping.

Makes 24

Think ahead: The shrimp can be grilled up to an hour beforehand. One way to save time is to buy precooked shrimp. Then all you need to do is peel them, leaving the tails intact. Squeeze them with lime juice and serve with the mayonnaise.
Variation: If you prefer to have a dipping sauce without alcohol, simply add 2 tablespoons of chopped, fresh herbs, such as dill, basil, or parsley to the mayonnaise instead of the tequila. Alternatively, add a teaspoon of grated lemon or lime zest for a fresh citrus flavor.

Petit Croque Monsieur

1 loaf of bread, sliced lengthwise
   into 6 slices (see Note)
$1/2$ cup whole-grain mustard
$31/2$ oz. thinly shaved, honey ham
$31/2$ oz. thinly sliced Jarlsberg cheese
$1/3$ cup very finely chopped mostarda
   di frutta (optional)
3 tablespoons butter
2 tablespoons olive oil

Brush each slice of bread with
1 tablespoon of mustard. Divide the
ham and cheese into three portions
and lay one portion of the ham, then
the cheese, on three bread slices. If
you are using mustard fruits, sprinkle
them over the cheese. Press the other
bread slices, mustard-side down, on
top so that you have three large
sandwiches. Cut eight rounds from
each sandwich with a 2-inch cutter.
Melt half the butter and oil in a
nonstick frying pan, and when the
butter begins to foam, cook half the
rounds until crisp and golden and the
cheese is just starting to melt. Keep
warm on a baking sheet in a warm
oven while you cook the remaining
rounds. Serve warm.

Makes 24

Note: Either ask your baker to slice
the bread lengthwise or buy an
unsliced loaf and do it yourself.
Variation: To transform the Croque
Monsieur to a Croque Madame, fry
24 quail eggs in a little oil and butter.
Then, stamp a neat circle out of the
egg with a 2-inch cutter. Place an
egg on top of each sandwich.

Hot

Mini spinach pies

⅓ cup olive oil
2 onions, finely chopped
2 cloves garlic, chopped
1⅔ cups small button mushrooms,
  roughly chopped
5 cups spinach, chopped
½ teaspoon chopped, fresh thyme
¾ cup feta, crumbled
1½-lb. pie pastry
milk, to glaze

Heat 2 tablespoons of the oil in a
frying pan over medium heat, add
the onions and garlic, and cook for
5 minutes or until soft and lightly
browned. Add the mushrooms and
cook for another 4 minutes or until
softened. Transfer to a bowl.

Heat 1 tablespoon of the oil in the
same pan over medium heat, add half
the spinach, and cook, stirring well,
for 2–3 minutes or until the spinach
has softened. Add to the bowl with
the onions. Repeat with the remaining
oil and spinach. Add the thyme and
feta to the bowl and mix. Season with
salt and pepper and set aside to cool.

Preheat the oven to 400°F and grease
two 12-cup, round-bottomed tart
pans. Roll out half the pastry between
two sheets of baking parchment and
cut out twenty-four rounds using a
3-inch cutter. Use these to line the
tart pans, then divide the spinach
mixture among the cups. Roll out
the remaining pastry between the
parchment paper and cut into 24
3-inch rounds to fit the tops of the
pies. Cover the pies with the lids and
press the edges with a fork to seal.
Prick the tops once with a fork, brush
with milk, and bake for 15–20 minutes
or until golden. Serve immediately
or cool on a wire rack.

Makes 24

Feta, arugula, and mushroom bruschetta

1 loaf Italian bread
1 large clove garlic, peeled
extra-virgin olive oil, to drizzle
1 tablespoon olive oil
1/4 cup butter
3 1/3 cups small portobello
  mushrooms, cut into quarters
2 cloves garlic, crushed
1/4 cup roughly torn, fresh basil
1 cup soft, marinated feta
2 1/2 cups baby arugula leaves

Preheat the oven to 400°F. Slice the loaf of bread diagonally into twelve 1/2-inch-thick slices. Lay the bread slices out in a single layer on a baking sheet and bake for 10–12 minutes or until they are lightly golden. Remove from the oven and rub the garlic clove over one side of each slice of toast. Lightly drizzle each slice with extra-virgin olive oil, then cut them in half again so that each piece is easily handled by your guests.

Heat the oil and butter in a frying pan over high heat until the butter has melted, then add the mushrooms and cook for 3–4 minutes. Add the garlic and cook for another minute. Remove the pan from the heat and stir in the basil, then season with some salt and cracked black pepper. Spread the feta on the prepared bruschetta, then add a few arugula leaves. To finish, top with some of the fried mushrooms. Serve immediately.

Makes 24

Note: Bruschetta are best made at the last moment to keep the bread from drying out or the toppings from making the bread soggy.

Sweet

Mixed nut tartlets

2 cups mixed nuts (e.g., pecans,
    macadamias, and hazelnuts)
3 cups all-purpose flour
1 cup butter, chopped
3 tablespoons light brown sugar
2 tablespoons granulated sugar
3 tablespoons light corn syrup
2 tablespoons butter, melted
2 eggs, lightly beaten

Preheat the oven to 350°F. Spread
the nuts on a baking sheet and bake
for 7 minutes.

Place the sifted flour and butter in a
food processor. Pulse for 10 seconds
or until the mixture resembles fine
breadcrumbs. Add about ⅓ cup
water and process until the mixture
just comes together. Add another
tablespoon of water if needed. Turn
out onto a lightly floured surface
and gather into a ball. Refrigerate
for 20 minutes.

Divide the pastry into ten portions.
Roll each portion out on a lightly
floured surface and line ten fluted,
3-inch tart pans. Trim any excess
pastry, then refrigerate for 10 minutes.
Put the pans on two baking sheets.
Cut sheets of crumpled baking
parchment to line the bottom and
side of each pan. Place baking beans
or rice in the pans and bake for
10 minutes. Remove the beans and
paper and bake for 10–15 minutes.

Divide the nuts among the pastry
shells. Whisk together the remaining
ingredients and drizzle the mixture
over the nuts. Bake for 15–20 minutes
or until just set and golden. Allow to
cool completely before serving.

Makes 10

Watermelon and vodka granita

2-lb. piece of watermelon, rind
  removed to give 8 cups flesh
2 teaspoons lime juice
¼ cup superfine sugar
¼ cup citrus-flavored vodka

Coarsely chop the watermelon, removing the seeds. Place the flesh in a food processor and add the lime juice and sugar. Process until smooth, then strain through a fine strainer. Stir in the vodka, then taste—if the watermelon is not very sweet, you may need to add a little more sugar.

Pour into a shallow, 6-cup, metal tray and freeze for 1 hour or until beginning to freeze around the edges. Scrape the frozen parts back into the mixture with a fork. Repeat every 30 minutes for 4 hours or until evenly sized ice crystals have formed.

Serve immediately or beat with a fork just before serving. To serve, scrape into dishes with a fork.

Serves 4–6

Serving suggestion: A scoop of the granita in a shot glass with vodka is a hit at summer cocktail parties. Variation: A tablespoon of finely chopped mint may be stirred through the mixture after straining the liquid.

Hazelnut biscotti with Frangelico shots

1³/₄ cups all-purpose flour
²/₃ cup superfine sugar
¹/₂ teaspoon baking powder
¹/₄ cup chilled, unsalted butter, cubed
2 eggs
1¹/₄ cups roughly chopped, roasted
   hazelnuts
2 teaspoons grated orange zest
¹/₂ teaspoon superfine sugar, extra

Frangelico shot
¹/₄ cup double-strength coffee
   (per person)
1–2 teaspoons Frangelico
   (per person)

Preheat the oven to 350°F and line two baking sheets with baking parchment. Place the sifted flour, sugar, baking powder, and a pinch of salt in a food processor and mix for 2 seconds. Add the butter and pulse until it resembles breadcrumbs. Add the eggs and process until the dough comes together.

Transfer the dough to a floured surface and knead in the hazelnuts and zest. Divide into two portions, and using floured hands, shape each into a log about 8 inches long. Place on the baking sheets and sprinkle with the extra sugar. Press the top of each log down gently to flatten slightly. Bake for 20 minutes or until golden. Remove and cool for 20 minutes. Reduce the oven temperature to 315°F.

Cut the logs diagonally into ¹/₂ x 2¹/₂-inch slices. Turn the baking parchment over, then spread on the baking sheet in a single layer. Return to the oven and bake for another 20–25 minutes or until just beginning to color. Cool completely before storing in an airtight container.

To make the Frangelico shot, pour hot coffee into shot glasses and top with Frangelico to taste.

Makes 40

Nougat

2 cups sugar
1 cup corn syrup
1/2 cup honey (preferably blossom
    honey)
2 egg whites
1 teaspoon vanilla extract
1/2 cup unsalted butter, softened
1/3 cup almonds, unblanched and
    toasted
1/2 cup glacé cherries (authentic,
    not imitation)

Grease an 11 x 7-inch baking dish and line with baking parchment. Stir the sugar, syrup, honey, 1/4 cup water, and 1/4 teaspoon salt over low heat in a heavy-bottomed saucepan until dissolved. Bring to a fast boil and cook for 8 minutes or until the mixture forms a hard ball when tested in water or reaches 225°F on a sugar thermometer. The correct temperature is very important, otherwise it will not set properly.

Beat the egg whites with an electric mixer until stiff peaks form. Slowly add a quarter of the sugar mixture to the egg whites and beat for 5 minutes or until it holds its shape. Cook the remaining syrup for 2 minutes or until a small amount forms brittle threads when dropped in cold water or reaches 315°F on a sugar thermometer. Add slowly to the meringue mixture with the beaters running, and beat until very thick.

Add the vanilla and butter and beat for another 5 minutes. Stir in the almonds and cherries with a metal spoon. Turn the mixture into the baking dish and smooth the top. Chill for at least 4 hours or until firm. Turn onto a board and cut into 1 1/2 x 3/4-inch pieces. Wrap each piece in cellophane and store in the refrigerator.

Makes 2 lbs.

Mini cherry galettes

22-oz. jar pitted morello cherries,
  drained
2 tablespoons unsalted butter
1½ tablespoons superfine sugar
1 egg yolk
½ teaspoon vanilla extract
½ cup ground almonds
1 tablespoon all-purpose flour
2 sheets frozen puff pastry, thawed
confectioners' sugar, for dusting
½ cup cherry jelly

Preheat the oven to 350°F. Line a baking sheet with baking parchment. Spread the cherries on several sheets of paper towels to absorb any excess liquid. Combine the butter and sugar and beat until creamy. Add the egg yolk and vanilla, stir in the combined almonds and flour, and chill until needed.

Cut thirty rounds from the pastry sheets using a 2-inch round cutter. Place half the rounds on the prepared baking sheet and lightly prick them all over with a fork. Cover with another sheet of baking parchment and weigh down with another baking sheet—this keeps the pastry from rising during baking. Bake for 10 minutes, remove from the oven, and allow to cool on the baking sheets. Repeat with the remaining rounds. Leave the oven on.

Place 1 level teaspoon of almond mixture in the center of each cooled pastry round, then press three cherries onto the almond mixture.

Bake for another 10 minutes or until lightly browned. Cool slightly, then dust lightly with confectioners' sugar. Place the jelly in a cup, stand in a saucepan of hot water, and stir until melted. Glaze the cherries by brushing them with the warmed jelly.

Makes 30

Hazelnut cream squares

4 eggs, separated
1/2 cup superfine sugar
1/2 cup self-rising flour
2/3 cup ground hazelnuts
2/3 cup unsalted butter, softened
1/2 cup chocolate hazelnut spread
1/2 cup confectioners' sugar, sifted
cocoa powder, to dust

Preheat the oven to 350°F. Grease an 8-inch, shallow, square cake pan and line the bottom with baking parchment. Beat the egg whites with an electric mixer in a bowl until soft peaks form. Gradually add the sugar, beating until thick and glossy. Beat the egg yolks into the mixture, one at a time.

Sift the flour over the mixture, add the ground hazelnuts, and fold in with a metal spoon. Melt 1 tablespoon of the butter with 2 tablespoons boiling water in a small bowl, then fold into the sponge mixture. Pour the mixture into the prepared pan and bake for 25 minutes or until cooked. Leave in the pan for 5 minutes before turning out onto a wire rack to cool. Cut the sponge in half horizontally through the center.

Beat the hazelnut spread and the remaining butter with an electric mixer until very creamy. Beat in the confectioners' sugar, then gradually add 3 teaspoons of boiling water and beat until smooth. Fill the cake with the icing and refrigerate until the filling is firm. Dust with the cocoa powder, then cut into squares.

Makes 16

Chocolate-dipped ice-cream balls

1 lb. ice cream (use vanilla or a
   mixture of vanilla, pistachio, and
   chocolate)
5 oz. dark chocolate
5 oz. white chocolate
5 oz. milk chocolate
2 tablespoons toasted, shelled
   walnuts, roughly chopped
2 tablespoons shelled pistachios,
   roughly chopped
2 tablespoons toasted, shredded
   coconut

Line two large baking sheets with baking parchment and place in the freezer to chill. Working quickly, use a melon baller to form thirty-six balls of ice cream and place on the chilled baking sheets. Place a toothpick in each ice-cream ball. Return to the freezer for 1 hour to harden.

Place the chocolate in three separate heatproof bowls. Bring a saucepan of water to a boil, then remove the saucepan from the heat. Position one bowl at a time over the saucepan, making sure the bottom of the bowl does not sit in the water. Stir occasionally until the chocolate has melted. Remove the bowl from the heat and set aside to cool. The chocolate should remain liquid—if it hardens, melt it again.

Put the walnuts, pistachios, and coconut in three separate small bowls. Working with twelve of the ice-cream balls, dip one at a time quickly in the dark chocolate, then into the bowl with the walnuts. Return to the freezer. Repeat the process with another twelve balls, dipping them in the melted white chocolate and the pistachios. Dip the last twelve balls in the milk chocolate, then the coconut. Freeze the ice-cream balls for 1 hour.

Makes 36

Grape fritters with cinnamon sugar

Cinnamon sugar
2 tablespoons superfine sugar
1 teaspoon ground cinnamon

2 eggs, separated
1/2 teaspoon vanilla extract
1/4 cup superfine sugar
3/4 cup seedless red or black grapes
1/3 cup self-rising flour
3 tablespoons unsalted butter

To make the cinnamon sugar, combine the sugar and cinnamon in a bowl.

Whisk the egg yolks with the vanilla and sugar until combined and just creamy. Slice each grape into four slices, then stir the grape slices into the egg yolk mixture. Sift the flour into the egg mixture. Beat the egg whites in a clean bowl until soft peaks form. Lightly fold half of the egg whites into the egg yolk mixture with a metal spoon until just combined, then repeat with the rest of the egg whites.

Melt 2 teaspoons of the butter in a frying pan over low heat. Place six heaping teaspoons of the batter into the pan. Cook over medium-low heat for 2–3 minutes, turning very carefully when the bottom becomes firm and bubbles appear around the edges. Cook for another 1–2 minutes or until golden. Remove to a plate and keep warm. Repeat to make twenty-four fritters. Dust the fritters with cinnamon sugar and serve warm.

Makes 24

Think ahead: The fritters are best made just before serving. If necessary, they can be heated in a 325°F oven for 5 minutes. Sprinkle with sugar after reheating.

Portuguese custard tarts

1¼ cups all-purpose flour
1½ tablespoons vegetable
  shortening, chopped and softened
2 tablespoons butter, chopped
  and softened
1 cup sugar
2 cups milk
3 tablespoons cornstarch
1 tablespoon custard dessert powder
4 egg yolks
1 teaspoon vanilla extract

Sift the flour and add about ¾ cup water or enough to form a soft dough. Gather into a ball, then roll out on nonstick baking parchment to form a 9½ x 12-inch rectangle. Spread with the vegetable shortening and roll up from the short edge.

Roll the dough out into a rectangle again and spread with the butter. Roll up again into a log and slice into twelve evenly sized pieces. Working from the center outward, use your fingertips to press each piece out to a circle that is large enough to cover the bottom and sides of a ⅓-cup muffin cup. Press into the cups and refrigerate while preparing the filling.

In a saucepan, stir the sugar and ⅓ cup of water over low heat until the sugar dissolves. Mix a little milk with the cornstarch and custard dessert powder to form a smooth paste. Add to the saucepan with the remaining milk, egg yolks, and vanilla. Stir over low heat until the mixture thickens. Put in a bowl, cover, and cool.

Preheat the oven to 425°F. Divide the filling among the pastry cases and bake for 30 minutes or until the custard is set and the tops have browned. Cool in the pans, then transfer to a wire rack.

Makes 12

Apricot and coconut macaroons

3 egg whites
1¾ cups superfine sugar
1¼ cups shredded coconut
½ cup finely chopped, glacé apricots
1½ tablespoons all-purpose flour
confectioners' sugar, for dusting

Preheat the oven to 300°F. Line a baking sheet with baking parchment. Combine the egg whites and sugar in a bowl and place over a saucepan of simmering water over low heat, making sure the bottom of the bowl does not touch the water. Whisk for 5 minutes or until thick and glossy. Do not overheat or the whites will cook. Allow to cool slightly, then fold in the coconut, apricots, and flour. Mix well. The mixture should be firm enough to pipe.

Spoon the warm mixture into a large pastry bag fitted with a ½-inch plain tip. Pipe 1¼-inch round mounds on the baking sheet, leaving 1¼ inches between each mound. With a wet finger, gently press the top down, to keep it from becoming too brown during baking.

Bake for 18–20 minutes or until light brown all over, then cool on the baking sheets. Dust the tops with confectioners' sugar before serving.

Makes about 45

Note: If you don't have a pastry bag, use a plastic bag and snip ½ inch off one of the corners; you will probably need to do it in two batches.
Think ahead: The macaroons will keep for up to 3 days if they are stored in an airtight container.

Baby coffee and walnut sour cream cakes

³/₄ cup walnuts
²/₃ cup firmly packed light brown
   sugar
¹/₂ cup unsalted butter, softened
2 eggs, lightly beaten
1 cup self-rising flour
¹/₃ cup sour cream
1 tablespoon coffee and chicory
   extract

Preheat the oven to 315°F. Lightly grease two 12-cup muffin pans. Process the walnuts and ¹/₄ cup of the brown sugar in a food processor until the walnuts are roughly chopped into small pieces. Transfer to a bowl.

Cream the butter and remaining sugar together in the food processor until pale and creamy. With the motor running, gradually add the egg and process until smooth. Add the flour and blend until well mixed. Add the sour cream and extract, and process until thoroughly mixed.

Spoon half a teaspoon of the walnut and sugar mixture into the bottom of each muffin cup, followed by a teaspoon of the cake mixture. Sprinkle a little more walnut mixture on top, add a little more cake mixture, and top with the remaining walnut mixture. Bake for 20 minutes or until risen and springy to the touch. Leave in the pans for 5 minutes. Remove the cakes using the handle of a teaspoon to loosen the side and bottom, then transfer to a wire rack to cool completely.

Makes 24

Chocolate brownies

$^1/_3$ cup all-purpose flour
$^1/_2$ cup cocoa powder
2 cups sugar
1 cup chopped pecans or golden
  walnuts
8 oz. semisweet chocolate
1 cup butter
2 teaspoons vanilla extract
4 eggs, lightly beaten

Preheat the oven to 350°F. Brush
an 8 x 12-inch cake pan with melted
butter or oil. Line the bottom with
baking parchment, extending it over
the two long sides.

Sift the flour and cocoa into a bowl
and add the sugar and nuts. Mix
together and make a hollow.

Using a large, sharp knife, chop the
chocolate into small pieces and add
to the dry ingredients.

Melt the butter in a small saucepan
over low heat and add to the dry
ingredients with the vanilla and eggs.
Mix well.

Pour into the cake pan, smooth the
surface, and bake for 50 minutes
(the mixture will still be a bit soft on
the inside). Refrigerate for at least
2 hours before cutting and serving.

Makes 24

Note: Use good-quality chocolate.
Baking chocolate is not suitable for
this recipe.

Baklava

Syrup
2 cups sugar
2 whole cloves
1 slice lemon
1/2 teaspoon ground cardamom

1 1/2 cups finely chopped, unblanched
  almonds
1 1/2 cups finely chopped walnuts
1 teaspoon ground cardamom
1 teaspoon pumpkin pie spice
1/2 cup superfine sugar
16 sheets phyllo pastry
2/3 cup unsalted butter, melted

To make the syrup, put the sugar, cloves, lemon, cardamom, and 2 cups of water in a large, heavy-bottomed saucepan and bring to a boil, stirring. Simmer for 12 minutes, remove the cloves and lemon, and refrigerate.

Preheat the oven to 350°F. Grease an 11 x 7-inch shallow pan. Mix the almonds, walnuts, cardamom, pie spice, and sugar in a bowl. Take four sheets of pastry and brush each sheet lightly with some of the melted butter. Fold the sheets in half crosswise, trim the edges so the pastry fits the bottom of the pan, then put in the pan.

Sprinkle one third of the nut mixture over the pastry, then top with another four sheets of pastry, brushing each with some of the melted butter and then layering, folding, and trimming.

Repeat the layers twice more. Trim the edges of the top layers, brush with melted butter, and cut into large diamonds. Bake for 30–35 minutes or until golden brown and crisp.

Pour the cold syrup over the hot baklava and refrigerate overnight before cutting into diamond shapes.

Serves 10

Lemon curd and blueberry tartlets

1/2 cup lemon juice
2 teaspoons finely grated lemon zest
6 egg yolks
1/2 cup sugar
1/3 cup butter, diced
4 sheets pie pastry (9 1/2 x 9 1/2 inches)
2 tablespoons confectioners' sugar
48 blueberries

Whisk together the lemon juice, zest, egg yolks, and sugar, then cook in a saucepan over low heat for 2 minutes or until the sugar has dissolved. Gradually add the butter, stirring continuously, and cook for 10 minutes or until thick. Remove from the heat and cover the surface with plastic wrap to keep a skin from forming. Refrigerate until needed.

Preheat the oven to 350°F and lightly grease twenty-four 1 1/4-inch tartlet pans. Cut forty-eight rounds from the pastry with a 2-inch cutter and line the pans with half of them. Lay the other rounds on a lined baking sheet, cover with plastic wrap, and refrigerate until needed. Bake the pastry cases for 12–15 minutes or until golden. Allow to cool completely. Repeat with the remaining rounds.

When cool, dust each tartlet with confectioners' sugar and spoon 1 teaspoon lemon curd into each. Top with a blueberry.

Makes 48

Think ahead: The cases can be baked up to a week in advance and stored in an airtight container. Before serving, heat in a 350°F oven for 5 minutes. The curd can be made up to 2 days ahead. Assemble the tarts no more than 1 hour before serving.

Fortune cookies

3 egg whites
1/2 cup confectioners' sugar, sifted
3 tablespoons unsalted butter, melted
1/2 cup all-purpose flour

Preheat the oven to 350°F. Lightly grease a baking sheet. Draw three 3-inch circles on a sheet of baking parchment, turn over, and use to line the baking sheet.

Place the egg whites in a clean, dry bowl and whisk until just frothy. Add the confectioners' sugar and butter and stir until smooth. Add the flour, mix until smooth, and leave for 15 minutes. Using a flat-bladed knife, spread 2 level teaspoons of mixture over each circle. Bake for 5 minutes or until the cookies are slightly brown around the edges.

Working quickly, remove the cookies from the baking sheets by sliding a flat-bladed knife under each one. Place a written fortune in each cookie. Fold in half, then in half again over the edge of a bowl. Keep a dishcloth handy to use when folding the cookies. The baking sheet is hot and you need to work fast, so be careful not to burn your hands. Cool on a wire rack. Cook the remaining mixture the same way. Make two or three cookies at a time, otherwise they will harden too quickly and break when folding.

Makes 30

Fennel wafers

¼ cup sugar
2 tablespoons sesame seeds
2 tablespoons fennel seeds
1½ cups all-purpose flour
¼ cup olive oil
¼ cup beer
1 tablespoon anisette liqueur

Preheat the oven to 400°F. Lightly grease a baking sheet and line with baking parchment. Mix the sugar with the sesame and fennel seeds.

Sift the flour and a pinch of salt into a large bowl and make a hollow in the center. Add the oil, beer, and liqueur, and mix with a large metal spoon until the dough comes together.

Transfer the dough to a lightly floured surface and knead until elastic. Wrap in plastic wrap and refrigerate for 30 minutes. Divide the dough in two and roll each portion out between two sheets of baking parchment as thinly as possible. Stamp rounds out of the dough using a 1½-inch round cutter; you should get about forty rounds.

Sprinkle the dough rounds with the sugar mixture, then gently roll a rolling pin over the top of them so that the seeds stick to the dough.

Transfer the rounds to a baking sheet and cook for 6–8 minutes. Put the wafers under a hot broiler for 2 minutes to caramelize the sugar, being careful not to burn them. Transfer to a wire rack and cool.

Makes about 40

Index

INDEX

INDEX

Photographers: Jon Bader, Cris Cordeiro, Craig Cranko, Joe Filshie, Roberto Jean François, Ian Hofstetter, Andre Martin, Rob Reichenfeld

Food Stylists: Anna-Marie Bruechert, Marie-Hélène Clauzon, Sarah de Nardi, Carolyn Fienberg, Cherise Koch, Michelle Noerianto, Sarah O'Brien, Maria Villegas

Food Preparation: Alison Adams, Justin Finlay, Justine Johnson, Valli Little, Ben Masters, Tracey Meharg, Kerrie Mullins, Kate Murdoch, Briget Palmer, Kim Passenger, Justine Poole, Angela Tregonning

Laurel Glen Publishing
An imprint of the Advantage Publishers Group
5880 Oberlin Drive, San Diego, CA 92121-4794
www.advantagebooksonline.com

All notations of errors or omissions should be addressed to Laurel Glen Publishing, editorial department, at the above address. All other correspondence (author inquiries, permissions, and rights) concerning the content of this book should be addressed to Murdoch Books®a division of Murdoch Magazines Pty Ltd, GPO Box 1203, Sydney NSW 1045, Australia.

NOTE: Those who might be at risk from the effects of salmonella poisoning (the elderly, pregnant women, young children, and those with a compromised immune system) should consult their physician before trying recipes made with raw eggs.

ISBN 1-57145-833-6
Library of Congress Cataloging-in-Publication Data available upon request.

Printed by Tien Wah Press, Singapore
1 2 3 4 5   06 05 04 03 02

Editorial Director: Diana Hill
Editor: Katharine Gasparini
U.S. Editor: Kerry MacKenzie
Creative Director: Marylouise Brammer
Designer: Annette Fitzgerald
Food Director: Lulu Grimes
Photographer (chapter openers): Ian Hofstetter
Stylist (chapter openers): Cherise Koch
Picture Librarian: Genevieve Huard
Chief Executive: Juliet Rogers
Publisher: Kay Scarlett
Production Manager: Kylie Kirkwood